PREVIOUS BOOKS

Healing by Contacting Your Cells.
Journal Excerpts From the Ring of Fire.
What Can You Do To Help Our World?
2013 And Beyond.
2013 And Beyond Part II.
2014 World Journals.
2015 World Healing.
2015 World Healing II

2016 WORLD JOURNALS

Barbara Wolf & Margaret Anderson

authorHOUSE®

AuthorHouse™
1663 Liberty Drive
Bloomington, IN 47403
www.authorhouse.com
Phone: 1 (800) 839-8640

Published by AuthorHouse 08/01/2016

ISBN: 978-1-5246-2117-9 (sc)
ISBN: 978-1-5246-2115-5 (hc)
ISBN: 978-1-5246-2116-2 (e)

Library of Congress Control Number: 2016912282

Print information available on the last page.

Any people depicted in stock imagery provided by Thinkstock are models,
and such images are being used for illustrative purposes only.
Certain stock imagery © Thinkstock.

This book is printed on acid-free paper.

This book is dedicated to Barbara's husband
Jack and to the rest of the world.

ACKNOWLEDGEMENTS

David J. Adams
Masami Saionji
Carmen Balhestero
Hideo Nakazawa
Hiroyoshi Kawagishi
Mitsuru Ooba
Kazuyuki Namatame
Fumi Johns Stewart
Paul Winter
Chief Golden Light Eagle
Grandmother SilverStar
Peter and Judy Dix
James Twyman
James Tyberonn
Stella Edmundson
Daniel Petito
Robert Ziefel
Emma Kunz
Judy Moss

FOREWORD

We firmly believe in what we believe, and we
realize you may not agree with everything we believe.
Probably we would not agree with everything you
agree with. But let us put aside our differences and
let us be friends.

It's the world that matters. Mother Earth needs help
and we are trying to give it to her. That is all that is
expected.

CONTENTS

INTRODUCTION

Chapter 1, as well as Chapter 9, the last chapter, tells you about the Solstice, an important event for Mother Earth. We are in New York City.

Chapter 2 tells you about the Spring Equinox, another important event during the year which Native Americans observe. Margaret and I were invited to attend this gathering at the Serpent Mound Spring Seed and Water Peace Summit. Our hearts were full of joy for having participated.

Chapters 3 and 4 find us in Australia to meet Aborigines and to learn about Songline energy stretching across the world to help bring balance and stimulation to Mother Earth. Also, we learn about Blessings Chimes used to stimulate peace energy in the waters and everywhere else.

Chapters 5 and 6 deal with our journey to Japan where we were Guests of Honor at an annual global event called Symphony of Peace Prayers (SOPP). We had other wonderful experiences such as staying in an ancient farmhouse and following traditional Japanese customs.

Chapters 7 and 8 will tell you about our adventures in Arkansas while handling the powerful energies of ancient Atlantean crystals. And, there is more. We were very busy in Arkansas!

Chapter 9, as mentioned in the first paragraph above, tells about the Solstice, and this one was the Summer Solstice. Again, we are in New York City, and we have exciting episodes for you to read. We hope you like our book!

CHAPTER 1

NEW YORK CITY

Joint Journals:

First from Barbara:

December 18, 2015:

2015 World Healing II, our last book, is finished and at the printers. The year of 2016 has not yet begun, but our 2016 book begins just now.

Why?

We want to tell you about attending musician Paul Winter's Solstice concert he has been performing yearly in December at the Cathedral of St. John the Divine, New York City.*

*See Glossary: Paul Winter.

Winter's main objective is to celebrate with optimism that at the Winter Solstice, the Light will begin to overcome the dark, a thought that has been with humanity across the world for a very long time. Here, in the Northern Hemisphere, the sun departs more daily until the Winter Solstice when it stands still for a moment before beginning its long journey toward the earth. At the Summer Solstice the sun is the closest to the earth for the year and it will begin its long journey to the darkest moment of the year.

At the Winter Solstice, Paul Winter says Happy New Year to the beginning of the return of the sun.

On December 18, Margaret and I take the train to New York City and we leave at a leisurely hour of 8:36 a.m. A taxi takes us to the station area which is a wreck. Big cranes are taking away the remains of a station that has been serving trains and passengers a long time. A small, very small temporary station has been built to serve customers until a big station is built. We are told this will be two years.

When we enter the tiny, temporary station, we see it is big enough to seat only a few customers, and there is little room for others to stand! FORTUNATELY, our train arrives on time and we stumble to the outside platform to board it. Those taking the train to New York City, its final destination, are told to board a car close to the front of the train, and this car is for us. We take seats on the right side of the train in order to have a good two-hour view of the Hudson River once the train turns south after we go through Albany.

As for our weather, there is no snow. Mother Earth has forgotten winter. I sit at the train window and look at the scenery as the train begins moving smoothly along. There are no leaves on the trees and so the scenery is not very inviting, but after we reach the Hudson, it is fun to look at this big, big river.

The river has little activity. I see only two big barges being towed northward, and I assume these are barges coming from Europe. I remember last year when the river turned to such solid ice, no boats of any type were using it. Will this happen this year?

I see only a few ducks and seagulls on the river, and I am hoping that the decision was to go South for the winter. Or, and I do not want to think about this, they have died because of poison put on the water to kill a rapid-growing water plant that has somehow found its way to the Hudson. It has been strangling the water.

I think of Pete Seeger,* America's famous folk musician who worked tirelessly to clean pollution from the Hudson River.

*See Glossary: Pete Seeger.

His boat, Clearwater, often has been seen on the Hudson and I see a boat that looks exactly like it. Helloooooooo, Clearwater. Helloooooooo, Pete Seeger, wherever you may be 'upstairs' in Heaven.

At New York Penn Station, the final destination of our train, we disembark and find ourselves with a great many at the station. Is everyone visiting New York City to buy Christmas presents? It is only a week before Christmas.

We maneuver ourselves to the proper place to take a metro to 96th Street and Broadway, and we are soon on our way to Day's Inn where we will spend three nights. This is a small, comfortable hotel and has the advantage of being close to the metro station we can use to go here, there and everywhere. Another advantage of staying at this hotel is to be able to walk three minutes to a very good restaurant, the Manhattan Diner.

December 19:

This morning we will visit the American Museum of Natural History, one of the world's largest museums. We have time to visit before going in the afternoon to Paul Winter's Solstice celebration at the Cathedral of St. John the Divine. The American Museum of Natural History is famous for paying attention to dinosaurs, and when we walk in, HELLO DINOSAUR! A big one is greeting us at the front door, mouth wide open showing HUGE teeth ready to eat something. Well, not today, Mr. Dinosaur.

We walk past him to ask a museum attendant where is the big crystal exhibit, and he begins walking with us, showing us the way. Soon we three are stopping in front of a skeleton looking like Lucy, the ancient old woman who certainly has created a lot of speculation over the years. She is with a male skeleton but we have little interest in him. Lucy has all our attention! Are we looking at the real skeleton? Last year we were at a museum in Uganda and unexpectedly we were standing in front of a skeleton called Lucy. Her skeleton was first spotted in Ethiopia only a stone's throw from where we were in Uganda.

And so, where is the real Lucy skeleton? In Uganda or in New York City standing in front of us? The museum attendant with us does not know, which means that Lucy remains a mystery to us.

We are soon at the crystal collection and it is large! Each stone is identified, but I feel like a stranger to most of them. I do not recognize the names. There are over 100,000 gems here, including diamonds, sapphires, rubies, etc., and yes, I do recognize these names, but there are so many I do not recognize. Mother Earth, I think you hide much of what is within you.

When it is coming close to turning our thoughts to our next adventure, the Winter Solstice at the Cathedral of St. John the Divine, we leave the museum by a 'back door' and take a taxi to the cathedral. It is not far, and on the way we are talking to the taxi driver who is from India and has been a taxi driver in New York City for 36 years.

When we reach the cathedral, a line has already formed outside its doors and Margaret and I know these are people waiting to seat themselves for the big Solstice celebration. We point out these waiting people to our taxi driver and tell him that close to 2000 will be in the cathedral from 2 p.m. to 4:30 p.m. Then there will be a scramble to find taxis.

Margaret and I join the waiting people, and when the doors open and the 30-foot line begins to move, we are soon inside the cathedral looking for seats. We do not have reserved seats, but the unreserved seating area has good visibility for the performance. At the end of a big row of seats, we sit, and there are bright stained glass windows only a few feet from us.

Yes! We have chosen well! Just when Paul Winter's performance begins, the sun comes brightly into the stained glass window and

4

shines directly on Margaret and me! Hello, sun, you have surprised us! We are happy you are shining on us!

Paul Winter's 36th Winter Solstice Celebration is called BRING HOME THE SUN. Well, the sun has heard and is responding. As I am writing you, I have in front of me a brochure from Paul Winter explaining that when the sun has moved to its southernmost point from the Equator, that is the moment of the Solstice, which means the sun is standing still. It pauses, and then it begins to return. Well, when we are sitting at his Solstice Celebration and the sun shines in the window, we feel it is at its southernmost point and it is acknowledging this to us! Wow!

This afternoon Paul Winter has with him Brazilian musicians, and among them are singers Renato Braz as well as Fabiana Cozza who, in 2012, was awarded the best samba singer. Joining their singing is traditional Brazilian drumming and instrument playing. Paul Winter, who has been a long-time friend of Renato Braz, fits in with all this. We in the audience are spellbound.

Similar to last year, gongs and bells and chimes accompany the music, and we watch as a sun gong climbs toward a stained glass window of the Christ wearing a bright red robe.

Then, to my amazement, a VERY BIG plastic balloon symbolizing the world with all its land and oceans begins to slowly rise until it is high up and close to the ceiling.

THE WORLD ASCENDS WITH ALL ON IT.

Optimism. Beautiful optimism. Yes, Paul Winter is an optimist.

The Cathedral is full bright when the program ends, and now he asks us all to sound like wolves. Today, 2000 plus howl. I do not know the significance.

After the performance, Margaret and I shake hands with Paul Winter who remembers us from last June's Summer Solstice.

December 20:

This morning, Sunday, our thoughts are on the Brooklyn Tabernacle and we will go there via the metro that is only two blocks from our hotel. I remember a few years ago when I wanted to take the metro early on a weekend morning. To my dismay, repair work was being done and the metro was very delayed. Will this happen today, a weekend?

Well, no. An express metro comes and for a couple minutes we are zooming before we transfer to a Brooklyn-bound express metro! Very quickly we reach Hoyt, the stop for the tabernacle.

But what is this? The terminal exit has changed. An employee seated nearby explains how we are to reach the tabernacle, and so we begin walking, knowing we will recognize 'signposts' from the last time. But, we do not see them! Why is this happening?

Males on bikes are carrying big plastic sacks containing empty beer cans and we are soon asking them for directions. They stop and politely help us. My memory recalls that few speak with them. Well, it is fun speaking with them, and I am actually happy that we became lost because it has given us a chance to speak with them!

And yes, we do reach the big, outer wooden doors of the Brooklyn Tabernacle. When we open them and enter, we encounter volunteers who have been escorting people through the next wooden doors to reach the big seating arrangement for the performance that is going on right now. I think probably 2,000 have found seats.

Margaret and I are escorted inside the auditorium and we walk no more than twenty feet to two available seats. One has a 'reserved' cloth on it and this is whipped aside for me to be seated.

WONDERFUL!

A full stage of singers as well as all the audience are lustily singing and we immediately join them. Above our heads are small TV screens with the words of the song we are singing.

YES! IT IS WONDERFUL TO BE HERE AGAIN.

We sing about ten minutes and then the audience seats itself to listen to the pastor who is on stage and ready to speak --- we think. Well, no. The pastor tells us to stand again, shake hands, and give hugs to our neighbors. And so we stand again to greet our neighbors. FUN. Everyone is smiles and smiles and giving kind words.

When we are seated again, in a boisterous voice, the pastor begins telling us about the Tabernacle's relationship to the community. This is Christmas time and there have been exciting events and more to come.

The day before, he says, the tabernacle has put on a grand celebration for homeless people living in shelters who were brought together for the celebration. From 6 a.m. to 6 p.m., 400 tabernacle volunteers worked with close to 3,000, greeting them, feeding them, giving them gifts and clothing. 700 toys were given to the children, and many had arrived in 50 school buses. When it was time to leave, some homeless children began to cry because they wanted to stay.

In addition to this amazing event, the Brooklyn Tabernacle delivered presents to 6,000 plus prison inmates. The pastor showed us a box containing what each inmate received -- a pair of socks, a toothbrush, toothpaste, comb, and a green t-shirt with Brooklyn Tabernacle lettering.

All of us in the congregation listen to the pastor and we clap and smile as he speaks to us about these wonderful events. We know this is the true meaning of Christmas. A giving from the heart.

The chorus at the Brooklyn Tabernacle begins singing and we join them. When Margaret and I leave, our minds are still on the great giving of this place, and we are full of joy and love for all that we have heard and seen.

We take a taxi to the aquarium at Coney Island, our next destination. Our attention will be on the big walrus we love to watch here as he splashes, dives under the water, then comes up just below us as we are watching. Did he survive Hurricane Sandy who drove the Atlantic Ocean into the aquarium destroying much in its wake? We ask when we arrive at the aquarium, and yes, the walrus did survive. His water home was destroyed and so rescuers found him a temporary home while a new aquarium is being built to replace the damaged one.

It is a disappointment not to see him.

We turn our attention to the Atlantic Ocean and the long span of white sand reaching out to the water from the boardwalk in front of the old aquarium. We walk to the shoreline and Margaret draws Vortex Symbols in the sand just at the water's edge. The last time she did this, the ocean came up to swallow the Symbols, and we know the ocean will do this again. Margaret watches to be sure her shoes and feet will not be swallowed.

She will tell you more about that. It is her turn now to write you about our wonderful trip to New York City.

From Margaret:

I am ready to energize the Atlantic Ocean with the Vortexes.* What are Vortexes? These are energy Symbols given to Native Americans Chief Golden Light Eagle and Grandmother SilverStar by the Higher Worlds to help Mother Earth, water, humanity, and everything on her during this time of change.

*See Glossary: Vortex Symbols.

It is cold today. I find it is too cold to walk in the water with bare feet. My heart walks in. I begin drawing the Vortex Symbols on the hard sand at the water's edge. When the plastic knife breaks, I use the blunt end to make strong outlines of the Symbols. In two rows close to each other, I draw twenty-two for the healing of the ocean, honoring the ocean and all oceans. I speak the name of each Symbol and when the Symbols are combined, I speak the name of the Vortexes formed:

Vortex of Light, Sound, and Vibration.
Vortex of Integrity.
Vortex of Symmetry.
Vortex of Strength, Health, and Happiness.
Vortex of Right Relationship.
Vortex of Growth.
Vortex of True Judgment.
Vortex of Perception.
Vortex of Connection to Life.
Vortex of True Nature.
Vortex of Love.

The ocean is happy and moves in to take the Symbols. They are all taken by the time we turn to leave and walk over the sand on our way to the subway to return to our hotel in New York City.

When we board, we ride along relaxed. There is no crowding and riders are diverse, attentive and kind. Most are young and busy with their cellphones. The older generation reads books or newspapers or sits quietly thinking their own thoughts. What a difference is riding the subway today.

As I sit quietly, I begin thinking about how Vortexes give Light. Here is channeling given to me from the Sun.

Welcome to New York. Your job is to bring back the Light to the city, to the planet. Humanity needs to greet each other in Love. There is no separation between the people. Their hearts are the same. It is the mind that pulls apart and separates. Bless this time of the Return of the Light – the sun in the Northern Hemisphere. The planets are with you. The universes are with you. We say, wake up dear humans to the many gifts given to you today in all the different dimensions including the 3rd. Smile – that opens the heart. Greet each other with a smile, a simple gift that will set Love ablaze on the planet.

A message of Light and Love from the Sun.

I love receiving messages from the Sun, and even when the Sun is not sending a message, I love looking up and focusing on what is far above me.

When Barbara and I began our journey to New York City to attend the Paul Winter's Solstice Celebration, I looked up and saw in the grey sky a long horizontal line opening up within a massive cloud formation. A line of brilliance suddenly let shafts of sunlight come to the ground. First there was only one narrow shaft and then came many shafts of sunlight to the land. I merge into the brilliant view.

Yes, on my train journey to New York City I felt very relaxed, then tired and ready to sleep. I had amazing dreams and one of them was with a beautiful golden retriever who shows me how dogs heal -- how animals heal. He took a gold ring of sunlight, a solid gold ring about 8 to 10 inches in diameter, and expanded it as healing energy to send to a person needing healing. So I knew how this healing is done, the happy dog did this many times. What a gift from the Sun and the Dog Kingdom!

I realize the golden retriever is a Sundog on earth -- a representative of the Sun's grace and joy on the planet. Afterward, I thought of other animals, such as the lamas connected to the Sun. I was thinking that the curved ears of lamas can hold an esoteric sun disc between their ears. I realized that humans need to wake up to the gifts the Sun gives daily -- the giving of unconditional Love ceaselessly to everyone, to everything in the Solar System and beyond.

I wake from my dreaming to realize the train is just outside Croton Harmon and the sun is shining brilliantly over the Hudson River, creating magnificent, sparkling reflections of the sunlight on the water. What an amazing gift to me, the viewer! And, I realize the sky has changed from grey to amazing bright sunlight to welcome us to New York City for the Return of the Sun -- the Winter Solstice celebration.

More channeling:

Enter the Sea of Love. New York is a teacher. It teaches the world that everyone can get along. All want to be here on these streets, in these buildings, seeing the life of the city – the stores, the museums, the shows, the sites. We, too, are here to see the Paul Winter Concert celebrating the Return of the Sun, the Light, Love shattering the darkness, fear and hatred. Today we celebrate Christmas coming, the birth of Christ, the giver of Light, the projector of Love.

The Christ has also channeled:

Be like me. Walk among the people who are your brothers and sisters. Give Light, receive Light. We are from the same Source. Earth can be heaven when one operates on the frequency of Love.

Approach others as you would wish to be approached. Seek the common base of understanding. Put yourself in the other one's shoes and walk around. Reach out in friendship.

Give a blessing of Love. We – you all live on the same planet. You share the same sunlight, the same air, the same oceans and rivers.

All of this belongs to the inhabitants of the planet from the fish to the Arctic bear to the elephant. Pull your self off being so special. Merge your boundaries into the whole. The tree gives oxygen, the land gives food and nurture, the oceans give life on the planet. The air gives the source of energy that makes the body work. See how these are to be cherished and maintained. Be mindful. Be open. Be thankful for this gracious gift of Life. Merge into the whole -- the Earth, the planetary systems, the universes, the one, the All – and then return refreshed. Things are not stale anymore. Life is vibrant. Live it to the fullest in joy. Let the mind release its tight reign and let the heart go forth to greet your brother, your sister on the planet, the home of everyone, everything.

With love eternal, the Christ.

Where there is Joy, I am there.
Where there is sorrow, I am there.
Where there is Love, I am there.
Follow the heart and the soul rejoices.
The Light comes out to light the planet.
This is the internal Winter Solstice Light.
Live in that Light frequency and we will be together in Peace.

The channelings from the Sun and the Christ have great affect on me as I am ready to attend Paul Winter's Winter Solstice celebration at the Cathedral of St. John the Divine. We take seats where we know we will have a good view of the performance. As we are waiting, the most amazing thing happens. Suddenly, a powerful blaze of light from the Sun comes in through stained glass windows and touches us. We turn, and everyone turns. The light is like a great spotlight. It shines and then flashes again and again. We realize the Sun is participating in the Solstice celebration while it is setting in its farthest southern position for the year -- at the Winter Solstice. We are sitting exactly where we can see/feel/witness this. Amazing!

When the Solstice program begins, I bring out the Vortexes and hold them on my lap throughout the welcoming of the Return of the Sun. A magnificent world globe is brought forward and hoisted above a gold spiral Christmas tree with singers and dancers skipping, leaping, singing around the tree.

I watch as a brilliant brass Sun Gong is slowly hoisted up to the stained glass window of the Christ wearing a red robe. While being hoisted, the Sun Gong is struck over and over again to shatter the Dark that has been holding back the Light. This symbolizes the Sun's return on the Winter Solstice, the day of the longest night, and the return of the Light.

The festive occasion of breaking the Dark is accompanied by Paul Winter playing his soprano saxophone as well as Brazilian, African, and American singers and dancers. When he ends the program, he gives out a fierce wolf howl and the audience, like a great wolf pack, enthusiastically joins him. The nature world and the human world have become one!

Amazing!

After the program, Barbara and I greet Paul Winter to tell him the event has brought great joy. We know each other and we are happy to speak with each other.

The next day:

It is very cold but there is no snow and we know the sky will be clear today. Barbara has written you that we make our way to the Brooklyn Tabernacle to attend a Sunday service. Here we join a full tabernacle to joyously sing songs of praise and joy and to hear the pastor explain about tabernacle volunteers serving 2,000 children and adults from local homeless shelters and foster care. 700 toys were given to the children, plus winter clothing, and 6,000 boxes of presents were sent to prison inmates.

Barbara has also explained that we visit the American Museum of Natural History to look at the crystals, the dinosaurs, etc.

It has been a good trip to New York City.

CHAPTER 2

SERPENT MOUND

Joint Journals:

First from Barbara:

Margaret and I have been invited to attend the Serpent Mound Spring Seed and Water Peace Summit at the Spring Equinox, March 18-20, and we will attend.* Native American Chief Golden Light Eagle will be in charge of this event. Who is Chief Golden Light Eagle? He is a Yankton Sioux, Dakota Spiritual Advisor and Sundance Chief. His first-class experience indicates that attending the seed and water summit would be an excellent experience.

*See Glossary: Serpent Mound Conference.

For centuries people have believed that the Spring Equinox is a powerful moment for growing food. Why?

It is believed that all has a consciousness, including seeds and water. As Dr. Emoto demonstrated to the world, positive energies will influence the growing of seeds into healthy food that, when eaten, will influence health in the bodies of humans, animals and birds. This influences the health of the world.

As for blessing water at the time of the Equinox, it is believed that this will bring health to the water. All that is nourished by healthy water is beneficial. Remember, between 80% and 90% of our physical body is water.

Also included in the ceremony at Serpent Mound is the attention to the need for health for Mother Earth. This health is within the framework of peace during this time of turmoil on her surface. Even without physically seeing peace for Mother Earth at the power place of Serpent Mound on the Equinox, nevertheless, the thought is there. All counts. Peace energy counts.

I would like to add here that at the Equinox, we all sing spontaneously Happy Birthday, Mother Earth. We want her to begin a new world of peace. The beginning of a new life.

Channeling from Margaret who asks for the significance of going to Serpent Mound on the Spring Equinox of 2016:

It is the beginning of Spring, the new beginning when the Earth has laid fallow to begin anew.

Layers and layers of histories are at Serpent Mound -- the meteor, the ancient rock formations, the ancient mound builders. At the Equinox, the new people, the awake people, the sleeping ones who are becoming awake will be there.

The Serpent manifests and energizes the power lines of the Earth. The egg in its mouth is the new beginning. The Earth-focused people are coming together to bless the seeds and the water -- carriers, initiators and preservers of life. Nutrients for humanity -- the seeds. Nutrients -- energy power for the Earth in the placement of the Serpent living on the crest over the creek near the meteor impact.

The Spring cycle brings those with new eyes, fresh hearts. The return of the Summer Light -- the growing season -- the full blossoming of Mother Earth. Humanity is more awake to honor the Serpent that holds the egg of continuing life and knowledge.

The ancient ones have returned to address their sacred spot. The Spirit Guardians observe and participate in the sacred ceremonies.

The people and the land of Serpent Mound are one. The people and the Earth are one. The people are united. The seeds and the water join them together. The Blessing Ceremony enhances all living things from specific to universal -- seeds, trees, roots, leaves, growing vegetables, especially corn.

The Equinox brings all life in balance. The planet is straight up with equal day and equal night. The moment of perfection.

*The Serpent marks the sunrise. It is a multiple ceremonial entity —
with Solstices and Equinoxes delineated. Wake up, humans, to honor the long history of being with the Earth. Stop and take time to be alive and fully present to the dance of Mother Earth and the Sun.*

Be awake and alive. Pick up the sensations in your body frequencies. Give Love. The Serpent is the door, an open door for more to be revealed.

From Barbara:

The Serpent Mound is located in the USA state of Ohio and corresponds to a crater made millions of years ago by the powerful impact of a meteorite. It is estimated that Native Americans deliberately shaped the mound to look like a serpent with its head pointing exactly in the direction of the Summer Solstice, another important Earth event. Investigators also estimate that the shape of the mound brings a strong correspondence with the constellation Draco (Dragon).*

*See Glossary: Constellation Draco.

The Serpent Mound was not used as a burial mound. Many Native American artifacts have been found here, such as numerous pipes (probably ceremonial), beads, pottery, arrowheads, etc.

For the 2016 Spring Equinox ceremony, Margaret and I and others will bring seeds. A spiritual woman from Hawaii had been invited to specifically bless the seeds, and her spiritual singing while blessing the seeds will be wonderful to hear!

On a visit to Hawaii, I learned that Hawaiian singing and dancing deliberately follow the movement of ocean waves coming to shore. In any case, my thought at the blessing ceremony will be that the seeds will be receiving special healthy energy from the Hawaiian woman.

From Margaret:

March 17:

To begin our journey to Serpent Mound, we must fly to Minneapolis, Minnesota to transfer to a flight going to Columbus, Ohio. Going to Minneapolis is a surprise. We feel we are touching base with the powerful energies of the headwaters of the Mississippi River. Our friends Judy and Peter Dix live in this area and they are authors of the book, Contact: We Are All One.* Many of the messages in their book are from Native Americans of their area telling about restoring the land to its original perfection.

* See Glossary: Contact: We Are All One.

I am carrying this book to Serpent Mound because I see the similarity of their words with the Spring Equinox ceremony we will be attending. I note the serendipity of all these connections.

On our second flight, Minneapolis to Columbus, Ohio, clouds below me catch my eye. One cloud is a Lenticular cloud with soft edges. What is this cloud? A dragon profile -- head and body! How amazing! Here we are on our way to Serpent Mound which is connected to the Draco constellation and the dragon cloud appears. Oh, my goodness!

We arrive late in Columbus and it is quite windy. We rent a car from Hertz and begin driving toward Serpent Mound in the vicinity of

Peebles, Ohio. At first, the traffic is heavy, but finally we are driving on less crowded roads in a beautiful countryside of hills and trees still in their winter mode.

Near Peebles, we stop at Woodland Altar, a spacious park with a pond and campground, lodges and chalets. At the main building we meet the management staff who are welcoming and kind. We are assigned accommodations at the Sugar Grove Lodge, a children's lodge, but there will be no children.

After Barbara and I are settled, we sit on the lodge veranda and watch the bright late afternoon sunset. It is an excellent time to draw the Vortexes for Serpent Mound which is over the next hill. I find a perfect place in front of a large pine tree cluster made from four trees combined. It is perfect in silhouette and balance. I draw the Vortex Symbols on the grass for the air, the water, and the land of Mother Earth at this special time, the Equinox.

The wind acknowledges special Symbols. Great gusts begin to blow as I draw the Symbols of the Universal Law of Free Will, the Universal Law of Change, and the Universal Law of Love. I smile when drawing the Spiritual Symbol of Equality, for this is the Symbol of Two Trees.

March 20 is Mother Earth's day of balance and equality. The Equinox.

We will be here.

March 18:

When the program begins for the Serpent Mound Spring Seed and Water Peace Summit 2016, it starts with drumming. We listen intently, and there are many of us from all over the country -- California, Hawaii, Minnesota, Wisconsin, Virginia, Connecticut, Missouri, New York, North Carolina, etc.

After the drumming, Chief Golden Light Eagle invites Barbara to be the first speaker and she is surprised. Eagle has not told her she would speak. She begins by saying we had expected to be in New York City at the United Nations to help ring the Peace Bell at the moment of the Equinox. Every year we are invited, but this year at this Equinox, we are at Serpent Mound to honor Mother Earth and the seeds and the water.

Barbara gives the microphone to Eagle who begins his talk by calling together women from the four directions, five races, and four colors -- white, black, red, yellow. An island woman from Hawaii is especially honored for coming here to this special ceremony. All are linked together by their enthusiasm and love of the planet.

Now a Native American traditional ceremony begins by honoring the four directions – by greeting the morning sunrise of the East, basking in the Sun's light of the South, saying good-bye to the Sun's rays of the West, and honoring the steady Light of Wisdom of the North.

This is followed by speakers focusing on the rebirth and rejuvenation of corn, an important food staple for humanity. We are told that ancient seeds are returning to bring nourishment to the people. This means ancient corn is being reborn into a new crop line. Special corn has been brought to the gathering and these seeds are passed around for us to hold. It is a joy to feel the presence of their power and their peace.

Just as we are holding the corn, we are told the Spirit Guardians wearing full regalia are here. They are pleased that humans are realizing the need to return to the original corn. During the winter months, corn is prayed over so when planted in the spring, they will grow robustly with great nourishment for the people. It is explained the Hopi during the winter increase the energy of their corn by praying over the seeds in ceremony in their kivas.

Now a speaker tells us about the sacred geometry of Serpent Mound and this connects directly with the Draco star clusters. *

*See Glossary: Ross Hamilton's research.

With interest, we learn that emphasis is placed on the presence of lightning strikes for enhancing and enlivening the corn and the water for the planting.

We know we and the attentive audience are busy learning about the sacredness of Serpent Mound as a revitalizer for earth, humanity, and the growing of spring planting.

Today is a perfect day for this. It is a bright day, and the trees are vibrant, the pond sparkling. The people are humming with happiness at being together with the like-minded who love Nature and the traditional way of growing corn and vegetables close to the land, and with the honoring of Mother Earth and all life forces seen and unseen.

March 19:

I address Serpent Mound to say Barbara and I are here to attend tonight the balancing of Mother Earth at the Equinox which is just after midnight. We are with you at your home with those who concentrate on the needs of the planet and all life forms. Will you speak?

Serpent Mound answers:

My jurisdiction is vast. My energy robust and enlivening – electric. Before entering my realm, you need to digest the concept that my mound system revitalizing the land exists in the next dimensions. Many fragments are still in place in the third dimension. My power lines are in place to be used when humanity gets off the material plane and onto the spiritual plane.

Later, I am feeling very close to Mother Earth and I ask her to comment on the loving people who have come to Serpent Mound, a place of extreme power, to honor the seeds and water at the Spring Equinox.

Mother Earth answers:

You are in the center of a meteor crater where energy is disjointed and yet powerfully monitored by the Serpent Mound moving energy through the body, creating music, running the scales of energy. The seeds everyone has brought will be energized to grow ever so sweetly and abundantly tomorrow.

I am vast. I am complex. I rejoice and receive the positive energy of humans who understand that my condition comes from constant affronts to my air, water and land systems. These caring humans are coming over the horizon as a force field for change,

The blind, unaware people take without replenishing. One system affects another. One action has a domino effect on the whole. The people gathered here are awake and concerned and work in their own way to help me, your Mother Earth.

Today, tonight is the Sacred Moment when I, the Sacred Planet, is in full alignment, straight up – equal day, equal night. A gate to spring in the Northern Hemisphere and a gate to fall in the Southern Hemisphere.

Balance, balance, balance for me and all systems. Rest in peace tonight with kind and caring people at this sacred spot. Blessing to those who carry Light in their hearts. They are aware residents on me, their planet. Joy and rejoicing. The UN Bell rings. The bells around the world ring. The drums sing tonight to echo my heartbeat.

With love, Mother Earth.

It is several hours after the exact moment of the Equinox and I am awake, focusing on Equinox prayers for peace and planetary healing. The energy of the Equinox links Mother Earth's heart, my heart, Draco's heart, and all the planets in the Solar System's hearts. There is a great sensitivity this day.

I watch the sunrise at 8:00 a.m. and the Equinox Sun is powerful. I know it is rising over Serpent Mound and I am now thinking of this morning's event, the ceremony of the Blessing of the Water.

When we reach Serpent Mound, and we assemble at a path that will take us take us to the water at the blessing site below the cliff where the Serpent rests. We are to stand beneath that cliff. We cannot walk there until after the arrival of Reni Aiai Bello, the Hawaiian spiritual leader who will conduct the ceremony. Native American Grandmother SilverStar, shaman and spiritual healer, will be with her.*

*See Glossary: Hawaiian Reni Aiai Bello and Native American Grandmother SilverStar.

As we wait, we begin to form a tight circle to sing Happy Birthday to Mother Earth. Yes, the Spring Equinox is considered to be her birthday.

Then one woman says her daughter's birthday is today and we ask for the daughter to come to the center of the circle so we can sing Happy Birthday to her. As we are singing, the daughter is so overwhelmed with emotion, she begins to cry.

Soon the Hawaiian shaman arrives with Native American Grandmother SilverStar. We watch as the Hawaiian Shaman asks permission from the guardians of the land to enter this sacred area to do ceremony. Yes, permission is granted.

Then all of us enter the woods to face the Hawaiian as she gives sacred prayers and blesses the water. When she sings, it is powerful and in total in harmony with the water. We know that all water is being affected in a positive way by her singing. We join in to bless the Serpent Mound and the water.

The Sun shines. Geese fly by in acknowledgement of the occasion. This is a sacred moment.

Later, the Serpent Mound channels again:

We are all one. We are made up of water. The emotions can churn up the internal waters or they can smooth into the pure love frequency. Love calms the water and brings up the heart line. If you are me and I am you at heart, then there would be no divisions.

Waters. Internal Waters. Sail in our boat on calm waters. Deep waters that open up to vast worlds of space, calm, harmony, peace.

I, the Serpent, am at home in both the water and on land. My speed and tranquility are always present. Today I rest on the land, above, receiving and modulating energies from all sources – above, below and within. I hold, I embody the electrical life force of the planet of creation. All life has this. The life force can be used for creation or destruction.

Prayer and meditation direct the life force in a positive, expanding way. That is why the seeds and water are brought to the Serpent Mound on the Power Day of the Spring Equinox.

Love can move mountains. Love can build cities. Love can calm waters. Love can create gardens, make trees grow, make all things thrive. Love enhances the Life force energy. Love is freely available. It cannot be taken. It is always there, the eternal spring well within the heart.

Look at the word 'spring'. So many meanings.

Spring = bubbling pure water sound.

Spring = the return of the growing season of the plants, trees, vegetables, flowers with the return of the Light.

Spring = to jump into action.

The day, this day, holds all these meanings.

People have gathered at my sanctuary and have received all these messages that are held in the deep waters of their being. You see what you can find when you still the mind and turn to quiet to receive my messages through the heart?

Serpent Lines. Lines move forward in a curving, undulating way. This is true of all Nature – water, the river lines, the vine lines, the wind lines, the breath lines, the Song lines. Love projects the song. The Serpent sings in its movement. The human sings with air and through the mind and heart. Let the voice be used for prayer and growing things. This is why people gather at Serpent Mound on Sacred Earth Days – the Equinoxes, the Solstices, and every day.

Go in Peace. Walk in Peace. Give Love to all you meet – human, plants, animal, stone, snake, planet and beyond.

The coil of the Serpent is never ending. It is creation energy.

Later, I begin grieving for destruction of mounds on the continent. I receive channeling:

Margaret, I see you grieve for the lost mounds – the breaking up of the energy enhancement of all this.

All creation exists at the same time. Present, Past, Future. The mounds and their dedicated task to enliven the strength of the land are always present. Tap into the knowledge and use the energy.

CHAPTER 3

AUSTRALIA

From Barbara:

Our intention has been to go to Australia in February, and we even had our plane tickets! United Airlines was offering free tickets if we had certain accumulated mileage with them and we did. Well, not exactly. Margaret was about 2,000 miles short, but United Airlines allowed her to drop the shortage by taking some of my accumulated mileage.

And then, at the last moment, circumstances are such that we cannot go. Fortunately, United allows us to postpone our trip and so we begin our journey on April 27, the day before my birthday. Our tickets show we begin flying to Australia on April 27 and we end our flying on April 29. No April 28 is mentioned. And so, good-bye birthday.

After we fly from the East Coast to Los Angeles, it is evening, and we settle down to sleep in our seats during our trip to Sydney, a 14-plus-hour flight.

But, oh dear! Just after leaving the California coast, the plane begins bumping and bouncing all over the place! What is happening? The Pacific seems unable to feel calm. Mother Earth, why do you feel so ill at ease?

I think of all the work Margaret and I have done to try to calm the Pacific. We have worked and worked with Aborigine spirits to ease tension at the plates where earthquakes happen.

The Aborigine spirits would play lively music with their didgeridoos and at the same time, we would listen to lively didgeridoo music coming from the computer. Yes, it was fun working with the Aborigine spirits! They would come in immediately to join us.

We know the Aborigines in Australia stem from a homeland in the great cluster of planets in the Pleiades. We know they remember this homeland, and recently we have received a notice that the Aborigines are ready to 'go home', abandon the Earth. One reason given is that the orchard is dry.

To us, this means that after taking over their land, Australia, by the White Man, living in Australia was no longer compatible for them. And so, they are returning home.

Well, we prefer that the Aborigines remain on the earth. They have a sensitivity as to how to treat Mother Earth properly, and this sensitivity is becoming sorely needed because of the great influx of others living here.

We are intending to visit the Aborigines living in Australia as a way of thanking the Aborigine spirits, and we want to ask them to remain.

When our flight crew announces we are soon arriving at Sydney Airport, I am ready to end the bumpy flight that has been showing us on the TV screen in front of our seats. Instead of a straight arrow going from California to Sydney, the arrow curves a bit to show the bumpiness of the flight. However, I must admit that as we come closer and closer to the Australian continent, the plane begins behaving smoother, more normal. Good!

I need to add here that when working to reduce the pressure at the Pacific plates, I have noted that as for the Australian continent, it has been exhibiting few earthquakes. To me, this means stability.

We arrive at Sydney Airport at 6:45 a.m. local time, and we take a taxi to a nearby hotel called the Stamford Plaza Sydney Airport where we are immediately given a room. We had phoned the hotel a few days ago to ask if we could have a room immediately when we arrive in the early morning, and answer has been YES. Hurray! We need to sleep after 27 plus hours of flying.

The next day, we are again at the airport, and this time we are at the domestic terminal of REX, Regional Express, to take a 7:30 a.m. flight to Broken Hill. For us, Broken Hill is IMPORTANT to reach, and so in order to not oversleep and thus miss the plane, we have left the hotel at 5 a.m. to ride a shuttle to the airport.

The plane taking us to Broken Hill is small, carrying not many passengers, and when the pilot takes us off the ground with a mighty roar, the plane begins to SHUTTER and SHAKE violently. It continues to perform in this manner throughout the two-hour trip. HELP! When we land at the airport, we are happy to leave the plane.

For whatever reason, when we first boarded, the stewardess said she would contact a taxi for us if we needed one and we said yes. Strange for her to ask about our need for a taxi, but of course cell phones reduce mileage to nearly nothing, and so she probably used one to phone. Maybe she phoned a family member who drives taxis. In any case, a female driver is waiting for us when we arrive at the airport.

This driver helps load our bags into her taxi, and when she starts driving to our hotel, the ibis Styles Broken Hill hotel, she drives slowly, like a tour guide, explaining about Broken Hill and its contents. We listen attentively.

At the hotel, our room is ready and we quickly leave our bags in the room in order to use an unmarked hotel door that, when opened, shows us the Broken Hill Visitor Information Center just a few feet away. By phone, we have been in contact with this center and when we asked for a hotel recommendation, this one where we will be staying has been mentioned. Yes, we are happy to open the door to find the two ladies we had been talking to over the phone. They remember us!

We tell them we need to find someone to take us to Sundown Hill at the setting of the sun, which, according to what we have read, is the best moment to be there. One phone call by the ladies brings an immediate arrangement for setting the time and the price for a tour woman to take us.

Now I need to explain why Sundown Hill catches our attention so strongly, but first, I need to say that we are calling this place Sundown Hill and others call it Broken Hill Sculpture Park. In any case, whatever the name, this place has to do with Songlines.

What are Songlines?

Well, we have been exploring various explanations and we still have questions. We know that Songlines are energy lines that travel across the earth and link with other traveling lines. In the former days of Australia, before the White Man made this continent his home, Aborigines dominated, as I have just explained. When the Aborigines traveled across this vast continent, they did not carry maps to show them where to go. They used the words of song to indicate their way. These words were energy lines, and the memory remains today.

The words pointed to landmarks involving the travelers, such as a big dip in the earth, or a waterhole, etc. It did not matter when a traveler found himself crossing land where people of other languages live. He would follow Songlines, energy lines.

This early concept of the Aborigines undoubtedly influenced Laurence Beck in the early 1990's to initiate a plan that sculptors from different parts of the world should gather at a place called Sundown Hill. This place, on the outskirts of Broken Hill, was considered to be one of the most powerful locations of Songlines. Here, he proposed that sculptors anchor a piece of their work. These sculptures would remain, and their energy would span the world to reach what is considered the most powerful energy point in the world -- Machu Picchu in southern South America.

And so, twelve sculptors from different parts of the world have planted their sculptures here. All are made from 53 tons of stones cut from sandstone boulders, and thus, the energy of the 12 sculptures begins the same.

However, because each sculptor is different and carries energy from his homeland, plus his life experiences, each sculpture, when finished, has this energy. Also, the energy from each sculpture runs in a different manner from Sundown Hill. Some energy goes underground and other energy goes above ground. Some go north and west and some go south and east. However, the end point is the same -- Machu Picchu.

Sundown Hill is of benefit to the world because the energy lines involve power and balance. For the benefit of the world, many, including David Adams and Krista Sonnen, are working diligently on energies related to Sundown Hill as well as to Machu Picchu.

About an hour before sundown, Margaret and I are in a car driven by a woman who has lived in this area all her life. As we begin riding along with her, a rural area, she begins explaining about her life here. We listen patiently and then we ask her if we will be seeing kangaroos when we reach Sundown Hill. Her answer is cautious. We may see some in the distance. And so, when we begin approaching Sundown Hill, a land with few trees, we scan the distance.

Look, I point out! Far to the right -- two, three, four kangaroos feasting on weeds or something. The tour lady slows the car while we look, and we even see a baby kangaroo with its mother.

WOW! WE ARE SEEING KANGAROOS.

When we reach Sundown Hill, we begin seeing the sculptures, and our tour woman parks the car close to several other cars. We know we will not be the only ones seeing the sculpting at sundown.

We walk up an incline to the first sculpture. It is standing by itself and all the others are standing by themselves. Here are the names of some of them -- Motherhood, Moon Goddess, the Ibis, Rainbow Serpent.

In the far distance, the sun is low, ready to part from us for the day. A series of clouds begin to interfere, and before the sun, which is red, has actually lowered itself behind Mother Earth, the clouds have interfered enough so we cannot actually see sundown.

Well, never mind. We are seeing the sculptures, and that is interesting,

It begins to be dark very quickly, and the tour lady puts us in the car to return us to the hotel. It has been a big day!

May 1, the first day of this month:

In the evening, we will take a flight to Adelaide and so we have today to look around Broken Hill. In the morning, we board a tour bus to ride around and see the sites. About fifteen are on the bus with us, and the driver, an experienced tour speaker, begins taking us to ancient mining sites.

We are surprised to see so many abandoned skeletons of mining structures towering above the ground. Probably these towering structures are to haul to the surface the underground 'wants' such as zinc and lead. The driver tells us that Broken Hill has the world's largest deposits of these two.

It bothers me that what is dug up and not needed is dumped at the surface with little or no concern for what it looks like. Big garbage piles of Mother Earth's below-surface goods.

We also learn that great numbers came to find work and there is a big Memorial built here for the 800 plus who died while mining.

After the tour, Margaret and I visit the Albert Kersten Mining and Minerals Museum which is just 'down the road' from the Visitor Center. We walk to it, and when we are nearly there, we realize the museum looks like a modest residence. Nevertheless, we enter and yes, it is a museum. Few crystals are displayed, although in one place there is a grouping of large crystals that seem to be enjoying being with each other.

Well, that's enough writing about Broken Hill. Now we are thinking about flying to Adelaide, but the plane does not leave until 7 p.m. We need to check out of our hotel long before that!

After we do check out, we take a taxi to the airport where we sit and sit and sit. It was not a busy place. When we arrive, a plane is ready to leave and after the passengers board, only the two of us, a cleaning man, and a uniformed director remain at the airport. The director asks us politely if we would mind him leaving the airport for a time.

Go, go, we tell him. We are comfortable and we need nothing. And so he takes off his uniformed jacket and leaves. We snuggle down on comfortable lounge chairs and sleep.

After a time, the director returns and he is all smiles. He thanks us and we feel he probably had returned home to be with his family. He says that when the plane comes in, we are to ignore announced boarding instructions and follow him on a shortcut to the plane.

When it lands, the plane looks the same as the one we took to Broken Hill from Sydney, and we hope it will not shake and shudder like its mate! We board and take our assigned places in the back. A few seat themselves in front of us but most of the seats are vacant.

The pilot takes us off the ground like a great shot and I am prepared for shaking and shuttering. Guess what!! None of that. The plane is steady throughout the one hour and fifteen minute flight. All in the dark. We cannot see lights until we reach our destination, Adelaide.

But now we face a difficulty. When we board, we are told our flight will not land at a terminal used by most other flights into Adelaide. David Adams will be meeting us. We have never seen him and he has never seen us. How will we recognize each other?

On arrival, we walk into a small waiting room that has only one person, a male, waiting to meet passengers. He is white-haired and he is wearing a bright, COLORFUL t-shirt. David Adams! * Yes, he is David Adams!

We happily fall into each other's arms for a big embrace and greeting.

Now that I have introduced you to David Adams, I want to tell you about him. From an esoteric standpoint, he is BIG TIME. A crutch is needed to help me explain about him, and this crutch will be his website.

http://www.dolphinempowerment.com/MarineMeditation.htm

* See Glossary: David Adams.

This is not a new website, but you will read about his involvement with the dolphins and other sea creatures and about his heavy involvement with crystals.

Yes, David Adams is BIG TIME for Mother Earth and all living on her. Just now, he is helping to drag our bags to a taxi that will be taking us to his home. We will spend two nights there and one full day before we fly to Brisbane to begin another part of our Australian journey.

By email, David has told us we will be at his house during the time when his esoteric group meets weekly. We are pleased to hear this because we want to meet his colleagues. Some are very involved with new energy stemming from the placing of 12 sculptures at Sundown Hill. All are involved with David's work with crystals for healing. In fact, during the early evening tomorrow at his home, crystal healing will be the main focus of a group meeting. He will give us crystals to hold while he speaks about this.

But just now, we are arriving at his home from the airport and having a short talk before retiring for the day. We tell him we have begun our journey the day before my birthday, April 28, and because we have crossed the International Date Line, there was no April 28. And so I had no birthday.

He looks at me and says, "My birthday is also April 28".

WHAT????? How often does one discuss one's birthday? Almost never. How often do we discover we have the same birth date as the one we are talking to? Never.

One time I was flying from Samoa to New Zealand and the pilot announced we were crossing the International Dateline. I was sitting next to a Samoan woman who was flying a short way to visit her family. I asked her what was her feeling of living with this dateline when every time she visits her family, she is crossing the dateline.

Her reply is brief. "Nonsense".

The gathering in England that developed the concept of an International Dateline certainly never conceived of what it would be like to be the Samoan woman sitting beside me who has to live with a date change whenever she flies a short way to visit her family.

In the morning, David drives us to the ocean where he and his group have often meditated for the water. When we arrive, the wind is blowing so strongly, we have to stay in the car. But, the scenery here in this part of Australia is beautiful and as we drive along, I see many houses, one after the other, facing the ocean. Yes, this would be a beautiful site to have one's home.

It was a long time ago when I last visited Australia, and today, 2016, I am amazed to see so many more homes. Of course the large number of cars today on the road is AWESOME.

Lunchtime finds us at a specific place what makes organic meals, and David's friends are already there to eat with us. A table is set for about twenty people, and we sit down with them.

I must say, the food is DELICIOUS. I can't even describe the taste, except to say again, DELICIOUS.

After the meal, Krista Sonnen begins driving Margaret and me, and we are stopping at a newly built ocean-side statue of Kuan Yin, Goddess of Mercy and Compassion. I am surprised to see this statue here. I was just as surprised when I was taken to her statue near Sao Paulo, Brazil. Her origin stems from Buddhism, and she has been worshipped for thousands of years, but one does not expect to find her in areas not dominated by Buddhism.

In Brazil, I like to visit her place which is a complex of a temples. Every weekend, in one of the buildings, doctors and other health people come to freely treat the people.

I do not know what the Australians have in mind for Kuan Yin, but I note that there are two small structures built near her statue. Probably at least one of them will be a temple for her. Maybe the Australians will some day do the same as the Brazilians -- have medical help freely available.

As I am writing you, I stop to Google the Internet, and I find there are a number of Kuan Yin sites in Australia. The one in Sydney seems very active.

In the early evening, when it is time for David Adams to begin his weekly group meeting at his house, Margaret and I are ready. The main focus for today's meeting is the work of the crystals. He hands each of us a healing Aquamarine crystal and he tells us to hold it in our left hand as he speaks.

He says the Aquamarine is very compatible with water, and I am thinking that our bodies are composed of about 80 percent water.

He tells us to slowly breathe in the energies of the crystal in our hand as we think about the healing of the crystal. Then we are to breathe slowly out of our body what we no longer want. We are to do this several times at his rhythm, and we continue as he speaks more to us.

The next day, May 3, Krista drives Margaret and me to the airport, and she stays with us as we check into Qantas Airways for our journey to Brisbane, a two-hour plus flight. In fact, Krista stays with us until we pass through Security and we are seated at the boarding gate. We leave at 3:35 p.m. and arrive at 6:25 p.m., and it is a comfortable flight.

When we arrive at the Brisbane airport, we worry about where we should walk to a bus stop to wait for a bus that will have a driver with our names on a ticket. His bus will take us directly from the airport to the home of Margaret's sister where we will be spending the next few days. Her house is on what is called the Sunshine Coast of Australia and Brisbane is inland with busy streets, etc., which Margaret's sister Stella does not want to tackle. And so, we have arranged for a bus to take us directly from the airport to her home.

How amazing are these arrangements! Instead of taking a taxis costing a fortune, we can board a bus with others and go directly to our destination.

But first, at the airport we need to find the proper place to board the bus. If we make a mistake, then, hello taxi costing a fortune. Well, worries are out the window. We ask an airport employee walking near us and he graciously changes his destination to walk with us to the bus stop just outside the front airport door. He shows us a posted sign giving the number of our bus.

We wait a very short time and the bus appears and the driver has a paper in his hands with our names on it. Then he loads our bags onto the back of the bus as we take seats in the front of the bus.

Australia, there are certain advantages to living in your country! Cooperative, friendly people live here.

About twenty others board the bus and soon we are traveling steadily along Brisbane streets. It is now quite dark and so shops have their lights on, which means we can see the merchandise they are selling.

In less than an hour, Brisbane has been left behind us, and then, quite soon, we stop briefly at a specific place where we passengers are sorted according to exactly where we are headed. We and our baggage are put in specific vans for the remainder of our journey.

Margaret's sister lives in Twin Waters, a retirement community of homes with separate house numbers. The driver turns into the retirement community, but now we have a problem. It is too dark to read the house numbers, and so he jumps out of the van and looks for help. We sit in the van waiting for him.

Very quickly he returns and guns his motor and we are off. Within three minutes we are at sister Stella's house.

Hurray! We are happy to stop traveling.

May 4:

A good night's sleep in this spacious place with different rooms for we three. Stella's two cats sleep with her, and the first thing this morning, BJ and Missy are the focus of our attention. We already know they are SHY and they hide under the bed when anyone is in the house except Stella. However, Stella has told us that in time they will become used to us, and so we try our best for them to be interested in us. No luck. They remain under Stella's bed.

We need to put our attention on water. We need to give the water big energies. With this in mind, Margaret will put down Vortexes at Mudjimba Beach, a popular resort close to the Twin Water retirement community. This is accomplished, and then, nearby, we stop on Baywater Drive at a cluster of trees close to the water's edge. A black cormorant is sitting at the water and we comment with amusement that he is waiting for us. Margaret slowly takes her Vortexes to the water's edge and the cormorant watches her. At a picnic table under trees, Stella and I watch Margaret as she puts down the Vortexes. A white heron appears on the water and at the same time a bird appears just over our heads to begin cheeping. And another. And another.

Little birds, babies, come to the ground to peck near us. A young magpie comes and a grey spotted dove. All seem interested that we three humans are here.

Do they know that our minds are on energy?

Yes.

What fun!

The next day, we go here and there with Stella and we do not see Aborigines. In fact, Margaret and I have seen none since arriving in Australia. Where are they?

We use the phone book to contact Aborigine places. Either no one answers the phone or a message says no one is available.

Why is this happening?

For whatever reason, my conclusion is that we are not to meet Aborigines.

Finally we have a solution. Margaret and I will hand-make chocolate chip cookies and give them to an Aborigine as a thank you for all the work the Aborigine spirits have done to cooperate with us when we have worked to help Mother Earth.

Stella is an excellent cook and she knows how to make chocolate chip cookies. She gives us the ingredients and then she tells us how to make them. Twenty-four cookies are what we want to make, and yes, we make them!

But now we must decide who will eat these cookies, and Stella has an idea. She knows of a place that may or may not become an Aborigine haven. It is located in the area of the Glass House Mountains and she puts us in her car to drive us over one hour to this place.

Glass House Mountains? What are these, Margaret and I wonder, and then we learn that they are a group of eleven hills that had risen sharply on the Sunshine coast millions of years ago and they remain to this day. They were formed by volcanic activity.

Stella move us along steadily and yes, we do begin to see what is called the Glass House Mountains. They are not sitting together, and each has its own name, but nevertheless, as a group they are called Glass House Mountains.

When we see a sign indicating we are about to arrive at a place that may pertain to Aborigines, Stella slows and then turns off the good road and onto a secondary road. Where we turn, and just above us is a house with a car and a dog barking. Most likely he is barking because he hears our car noises. We follow the secondary road only a short time and then we realize we should have stopped at the house. And so we turn around and enter its driveway. A man comes from the house and we tell him we are looking for the place where Aborigines gather.

His reply gives us hope for the cookies. Tomorrow, he says, Aborigine women will be here to discuss matters.

Hurray! They will get the cookies!

We take the cookies out of the car and give them to the man while we explain that we want to thank the Aborigines who maintained for years and years and years this continent called Australia. He is pleased and he says tomorrow the Aborigine women will get the cookies.

In the distance, directly behind where this man is speaking to us, is one of the Glass House Mountains. I point this out to him and tell him that this Glass House Mountain is his guardian. He nods his head. He understands.

In any case, the 'thank you' cookies will be eaten by Aborigines! We climb back into the car, all smiles, wave good-bye to the man and his dog, and we return to Stella's home.

Stella has one more long ride for us in the car and she does not tell us where she will be taking us. As she drives, Margaret and I look at the beautiful scenery. Again, we begin to climb, and after quite a long journey, unexpectedly, Stella stops at a place called The White Eagle Lodge.

We leave the car amazed at what we are looking at – a stately, beautiful building that looks like a spiritual center. Indeed, we learn that this is a spiritual and healing center open to all who agree with its teachings.

What are its teachings? White Eagle,* who has been the source of channeling for seventy-plus years, believes all should have a loving heart and inner peace as well as all should live in peaceful brotherhood with each other. Via channeling, his method of healing has been adopted -- the laying on of hands and also group distance healing.

*See Glossary: White Eagle.

Today there are White Eagle Lodges in a number of places around the world -- the USA, England, Scotland, Australia, Africa.

When we enter the Australian Lodge, we are met by two devotees, and they are ready to begin meditation. Do we wish to join, they ask? Yes, of course, and we enter a beautiful room to meditate. The Light is powerful in this room, as is the Light in all the Lodge and beyond.

After the meditation, I look at books explaining about White Eagle teachings, and I want to buy one of them. It is given to me without payment and explained that it will be mailed to me. And yes, it arrives at my house about a week after I return.

Interesting, in 1997 I receive a phone call from a stranger, a woman in California who hesitantly explains that she has received channeling from White Eagle who says the channeling is for me. Can she send it? Yes, of course, and she does.

I had never heard of White Eagle, but he obviously had heard about me. I had just begun the Global Meditations Network, which quickly became a world wide network, as the wording indicates. White Eagle's channeling explained techniques on how to handle negativity. The California woman sent two pages of writing from the channeling.

And so now, 2016, suddenly I am taken to a Lodge, a White Eagle Lodge in Australia that is under the guidance of White Eagle.

Before leaving Australia, Margaret's sister Stella takes us to the Australia Zoo. We will see kangaroos close-up, and we will FEED THEM with our own hands.

A number of kangaroos are interested in being fed. We are shown how to properly offer food on a flat hand, palm up, so the kangaroos will eat from us. Sure enough! We put food on our palms and offer them in a proper manner, and the kangaroos do not hesitate to begin eating gently from our hands. Amazing!

We are with them inside their enclosure, which does not look like an enclosure because it is big. Some are standing and eating from us and others are lying down and resting. Maybe their stomachs are full and they are not interested in more food just then. There are large kangaroos and mother kangaroos and babies. None are afraid of us.

When we leave the kangaroos, we come to an extensive, treed area where there are many types of birds. Again, they are not afraid of us. They swoop down and some touch our heads. Maybe they are also wanting us to give them food. Well, the kangaroos have eaten all the food we had to offer.

I need to mention here that when we first reach zoo residents, we stop at an enclosure that has the largest turtles in the world. And yes, they are BIG. One is a male and the other is female. They seem to like each other. As we are watching, the female slowly crawls to the male to give him a kiss near the mouth.

May 11:

Today, we leave for Japan.

We are up early at Stella's house to be ready for a 5:20 a.m. van pickup to take us to a bus driving us to the Brisbane airport.

We have been worried about the van pickup in the dark. Will the driver know how to reach Stella's house? We remember the problem a week ago when the van driver could not read the numbers for the retirement houses.

Yesterday, we phone the bus company not two but three times because of our worry. And today, Stella, in order to help matters, walks in the dark in the direction of where the bus should be arriving.

Well, we need not have worried. When the bus company realized our worry, a separate van was ordered for us. Stella and the van are soon at the front of her house and we are loading our bags into the van. All problems solved!

The driver drops us off at the gathering place for bus riders to the airport and soon we are on our way. Traffic is light at this hour, and we move along smoothly. Daylight begins to help us.

At Brisbane Airport, we are given directions for finding the Qantas Flight taking us to Narita, Japan. Just after 10 a.m. we are in the air and our pilot is flying us through a cloudless blue sky to our destination. In fact, the weather is so good, we arrive early at Narita, about a five-hour journey.

CHAPTER 4

AUSTRALIA

From Margaret:

April 27:

Barbara and I begin a long 27-hour journey by air to Sydney, Australia. We are comfortable enough and we sleep most of the time.

Outside Hawaii, Barbara wakes me. Our flight has become rough and choppy. Peace, Love and Light is needed. For the stability of the Pacific, I do the Vortexes first for the entire Ring of Fire, the Pacific, concentrating on the plates, focusing on the guardians of the plates. Near Apia, Samoa, the plane flies somewhat off course. Hummmmmm. What does this mean? Mother Earth tension.

When we arrive in Sydney, we take a shuttle to the Stamford Plaza Sydney Airport Hotel where we rest and sleep. I can feel the stability of Mother Earth here. I send my love frequencies to the land and to the trees and to the birds, the dolphins and whales.

I announce our arrival to the Aborigine Spirits, thanking them for their work.

They say: *Welcome to Australia, the oldest land, stabilizer for Earth's surface and beneath. We walk carefully as we are going, connecting to the frequencies of life forms present, past and future. We carry deep soundings to the land and to the Spirit of All Being. We greet you and we are aware of our place in the whole life system. We are not grand and puffy. We are quiet and discrete, carrying a great heart and appreciation for the intricacies of Nature's systems.*

Skill is being in tune with that which we are focused. We are aware of your concern for the moving of the tectonic plates in a sharp, abrupt way that can cause damage to building structures and possible loss of life.

All need to find a doorway to enter Australia. You have selected Broken Hill (Sundown Hill) as a doorway to enter Australia because here is the merging of the Songlines with each other. Crystals are very much involved. Your heart is your geiger counter sensor. Let it be quiet to receive messages and connections. Sundown Hill at Broken Hill, like Grand Central Station, is a power station where line energies come in and go out.

Take the understandings one at a time. Do not be overwhelmed. Australia spreads out a calm, positive frequency of stability. Tap into it. You felt it this morning coming in by plane. You rode that frequency as you would ride a great wave, a swell of joy underneath. Peace and Harmony. Joy and Oneness.

The mass media (movies, TV, rugby games) divides into teams and wrestles with opposing forces. Since All is One, and we are all One, why would one struggle against One's self? We are all a part of the whole, a beam of light, a dot on the surface of the land, a flower, a crystal, a breath. Energy. We are energy. Walk with peace among peoples, among the fluid environment, the air, the stone environment.

If you have mastered one inch of the land, then you have mastered the whole of All. Put the mind aside. It wants to run all over the place. Sit and be with one place at our own campfire. You walk many lines. See what gifts appear.

You carry Vortex Symbols of Galactic harmony. In gratitude for this amazing planet/star, you carry the desire to help Mother Earth exist and grow harmoniously and abundantly in peace and joy.

The Higher Worlds are helping. Follow their advice. The planets and the planetary systems are aware of Earth's change and ascension.

Ascension means expansion – taking in the whole – appreciation of all life forms and energy systems. That is why Aborigine art is so vibrant. It captures the vitality of life expressed in an energy way. Energy is our signature. Vibrancy is caught in one dot, one curved line. X-ray eyes see the energy structure.

Because of your work with energy, you have chosen to go to Sundown Hill, a powerful Songline energy place of stone and art sculpture linked to the entire world. You bring the whale-dolphin water lines and bird flight lines. Each a singer; each a Songline in their own being.

The native indigenous people (Aborigines) know these lines as the trees know their lines. Both are rooted deep into Mother Earth -- receptors of the Sun and Cosmic Light.

We are playing with expanding your heart lines. You love surface patterns. You love the deep rocks. Everything here is to be seen and felt with the heart. Welcome to Australia, the solid ancient land and the solid ancient people.

We will meet you. In gratitude for this opportunity.

With love from the Aborigine Spirits.

April 30:

Today we fly to Broken Hill and when we arrive, we quickly arrange to have someone take us in the early evening to Sundown Hill. This is the best time to be there. When the sun sets, the power energizes the land, and so we will be there at the best time of the day.

We are being driven through a beautiful landscape of peace. The land is totally of Nature. We even see kangaroos -- large ones and little ones. It is their time to be out and about. It has rained and there is a freshness to the air.

We are soon at Sundown Hill, and with fascination, I am looking at vertical rock layers pointing upwards. I also see sculptures that I know hold the Songlines. There are twelve in all.*

*See Glossary: Broken Hill Sculptures.

Above me I see a lion in the clouds reminding me of the Christ lion painted by Glenda Green.* I also see a grey, heart-shaped cloud reminding me of Sakurajima's cloud of volcanic steam formed in a heart shape that was a parting gift given to us when we visited Japan in 2004.

*See Glossary: Glenda Green, The Lamb and the Lion.

At the far horizon in the clouds, I see the silhouette of a horse with the fire of the sunset inside him. I call him the Fire Horse. He reminds me of the Nazca line design in South America. I realize that I have a link here between the two -- the Fire Horse of Australia and the Nazca Lines of South America. I realize that cloud formations link our minds to different areas in the world.

Later, I receive channeling:

The sky was throwing symbols to you.

What do the symbols mean, I ask?

The cloud maker and the viewer combine psychic forces to produce images, symbols, aspects to think about, lines to follow. Sky-drawing lines, forms, open up topics.

We suggest you first ask permission to delve into the heart of these mysteries. You are on sacred land and you need to ask the Keepers of the Region. This is a complex land with all its aspects – Songlines.

histories, energy lines that nurture Mother Earth and are guarded by the lizard and the kangaroo and the Aborigine Spirits.

I say my heart is open and ready to receive.

The channeling continues:

We are in ceremony. Walk and sit at our fire. The great rainstorm welcomed your visit. Mother Earth spoke. Great nutrients were showered upon the land.

The Sun and the clouds, water vapor, Spirit Guardians, played and danced the day. You watched the sunset and reacted not with disappointment that the sun descended behind a cloudbank.

Now the Songlines speak:

You do no need to see the Sun to feel the power of the sunset and the power of Sundown Hill. Our power continues in all weather conditions. Sun shining, rain, fog. Energy is energy enhancing Mother Earth. Her psychic blood flows through her arteries. The coming in and going out and coming in and going out in the rhythm of Mother Earth's heartbeat.

The lines are all around, deep below the surface of the earth. They come closer to the surface here. The sculptures, energetic caps, filter and project concepts and stories.

Kangaroos were here eating and watching. Human line dancers came as a group. Your guide was one of them. What are dancers? They put the concept of joy into movement. When you dance and your heart is in line with the planet, you become part of the flow of energy.

You came with all your connections, traditions, lines. You travel the world. You are focused on the earth plates. You have asked for balance and you have been introduced at Sundown Hill to the Cosmic Balancers that work with universal Songlines.

The power of Sundown Hill are the rocks and geological formations. Look at the vertical rock layers, not resting as deposited but turned up on their ends. Power shifts and rocks uplift happen and yet the Songlines continue here and are enhanced.

Earlier, when you were in Japan, you felt the Guardian presence of the volcanic mountain of Sakurajima. His guardian energy gave you a message in ancient calligraphy. You saw the guardian as an artist wearing a black headband when writing in calligraphy for you. As a farewell greeting he gave you a heart-shaped cloud. Today at Sundown Hill, you saw the same heart-shaped cloud.

———————————

I knew this was a link of energy from Sundown Hill to Sakurajima, Japan.

The Songlines continue channeling:

Today at Sundown Hill, you saw the lion in the sky here, a direct image of the Christ Lion of artist Glenda Green. This image shows that the fierce will lie down with the weak, the lion and the lamb. This indicates that the fierce Nature forces can be modified, made soft to be in cooperation with weaker forces. When asked by love, animals can join together in peace.

The cloud people used your mind to catch visual images projected in cloudbanks. Great forces, weak forces can blend together in balance and peace.

Barbara spotted the spaceships that were above the clouds yesterday when your plane was descending to land at Broken Hill. The ships were there, within the clouds, caught by the sunlight, disguised as unusual clouds above the clouds.

The scenes have been alive with messages and possibilities.

When the big rain came, pouring buckets of water on the land, it was a blessing for the land. With water, the flowers will grow, the grass will be green, the trees will rejoice with growth.

With love from the Keepers of the Land.

I reply: Thank you for your insight.

Their response: *Thank you for listening. Come rest again. Feel the hmmmmmmm of the energy current traveling here and there around the world. Long lines and short lines and cosmic lines. Australia, yeah!*

We wish to add here that cats are great picker-uppers of energy lines. Songlines. They sleep, they travel, they return. Dogs are sensitive but more in tune with their keepers.

Dolphins and whales are great singers, sounders and balancers of energy lines, Songlines. Their presence uplifts the energy. They are to be cherished and revered.

Also, consider circles and lines of the spider web. These are lines of pearls, lines of song, histories, present and future. The lines carry the power and the circles distribute the calm energy for the benefit of balance and moderation.

More channeling.

The lizard that ran near the road catching many flies, bugs, and insects is an aspect of the dragon and Dragon Lines.

I ask, are Dragon Lines and Songlines connected?

The answer: *Sometimes yes and sometimes no. Mother Earth has multiple energy systems. The dragons are Keepers and Guardians of the water veins. They bring positive benefit for the seasons. The dragon, often holding a pearl, indicates wisdom to be used for understanding. Dragons are nurturers of life force.*

May 1:

8:45 a.m., we join a bus tour of the city of Broken Hill which shows us neighborhoods, schools, churches, miners' houses, old hotels, old bars. On a long ridge are old mines with dark wooden mineshaft structures. Great slag heaps are found here.

When the bus stops for us to walk around a mine complex, many go to the mine shafts. I go to the outcrop of the original rock bed that led to all this mining. I put my hands on this to send love and healing to the entire region.

I am remembering the gold mine in Sao Tome das Letras, Brazil, where we visited a Sun Disc and listened to the angelic music, Musical Rapture.* There, because of our meditation, the deep caverns of the gold mines were transformed into energy resembling the energy of a great cathedral. The rocks held the frequencies.

*See Glossary, Musical Rapture.

At Broken Hill, I draw on the rock's surface Vortex Symbols of the Universal Law of Nature, the Spiritual Law of Protection, the Universal Law of Love, and the Spiritual Law of Healing.

When all have returned to the bus, the tour director takes us to a memorial to miners who lost their lives in the mines. When leaving the memorial, I sound the OM's (a healing sound) to send healing to the people and the land. Grief and sadness come to me.

When the tour is finished, Barbara and I go to the Broken Hill Tourist Center to ask to see stones. Here, I see for sale a small bright shiny stone of silver, lead, zinc ore. Immediately I love it, but the mining sadness stops me from buying it. This stone would bring sadness home to me.

Now Barbara and I walk to a nearby geological museum, Broken Hill Mining & Minerals Museum, GeoCentre located at the corner of Crystal and Bromide Streets.* We watch a FANTASTIC film presentation on the creation of the rock deposits of this area. This film covers a great span of time from the earliest volcanic activity to now. It brings everything together.

*See Glossary: Broken Hill Mining & Minerals Museum.

We walk among the crystals and Barbara says that under this entire area is POWERFUL BEDROCK and this is what enhances the Songlines and the Sculptures. The Crystals and the Songlines are one! YES! It all makes sense — today's sad trudging among mining towers and slag heaps fades away. I can buy the rock piece that wanted to come with me.

As I write you, he sits beside me at my computer.

We are all one, he says.

May 2:

Last night we flew to Adelaide, and now we are at the home of David Adams, healer and channeler who puts continuous focus on marine meditations for oceans.*

*See Glossary: David Adams.

Just now it is very early in the morning and I have shifted my attention from the outback to the water at a point where the land and the ocean meet. David Adams lives near the ocean.

I am ready to connect to the dolphins now that I am within their of influence. I say to them, I send you my greetings and love. I am still in transition from the strong influence of the Songlines. Do you have comments?

The Dolphins respond: *Margaret, you are swimming in vast territories, dimensions of David Adams' realm which expands through elements, dimensions and time. Relax and go with the flow. There are no rocks, no barriers. The rocks are crystal light. The guidance is through your heart. Each thought is a possibility to follow a pathway to a new discovery. Enjoy this time. Do not hold on too tightly. Dolphins cannot swim holding on. Expand. Expand. Expand. You are beyond Australia when you are in the realm of David.*

The Broken Hill area was specific and global and cosmic. The key points are the land, the Songlines, the surface. Put away the surface and go into the energy. See what Mother Earth wants. Give her your frequency of Love that sustains her and she sustains you. The land sustains you, the water sustains you, the air sustains you, the fire sustains you. The Masters, the allies, your friends in the Higher Worlds, sustain you. Go with your butterfly net and catch the understanding of the wonders of the coming together.

With love from the Dolphins.

This morning David Adams drives us to Moana Beach where he has held marine meditations for many years for the healing of the oceans. The wind is so intense, we remain in the car and do not walk on the beach. Then he begins driving us along breathtaking coastal scenery to Port Noarlunga where we have lunch with David's friends at Agatha's food store.

The food is delicious and we have wonderful conversation. Everyone has a same deep interest in Earth healing, healing the oceans, Songlines of Sundown Hill, crystals, on and on. We will be meeting this group again for their Monday night gathering.

After lunch, Krista Sonnen and Kath Smith take Barbara and me further down the coast to see the magnificent tall statue of Quan Yin at Sellicks Hill. The statue is 18 meters high (about 60 feet tall) and she represents the Lady of Compassion blessing the people and pouring the sacred pure water. I stand in front her for a moment to make eye contact. The wind is still blowing fiercely.

In the evening at David's house, we gather with his group in a meditation circle and we feel very honored to be here at this moment. We each hold an aquamarine crystal as we listen to David's message from Aquamarine of the Spirit of Crystals and Gemstones. It is a deeply moving moment.

Now David presents me with a gift of the original Blessings Chimes he has constructed following the instructions of Saint Germain. Over the years, David has used these Blessings Chimes for the Marine Meditations.

I am overwhelmed and deeply touched by his gift, which holds the frequencies of Sound, Light and Water. I will continue to use these Blessings Chimes to heal Mother Earth's waters.

More channeling to me:

All life forms are energized with love. It is love that propels the Songlines. It is love that the crystals send out with their light. It is love that Mother Earth sends to space and beyond.

The Blessings Chimes hold the love frequency with its sound and movement. Use them because it has been a gift to you to expand Light and Love. These frequencies come out when there is a feeling of peace and welcome. The birds sing to grow the plants and trees. The Blessings Chimes sing to grow the life force of the oceans. Carry them with you. It is a sacred gift.

May 3:

We are taken to the Adelaide Airport to fly to Brisbane where we will board a shuttle bus to go north to the Sunshine Coast, location of Twin Water retirement community where my sister Stella lives. We are excited to be with Stella. She is a wonderful sister. When we arrive we see she lives in a beautiful home with two cats.

May 4:

The first morning with Stella, she drives us to Mudjimba Beach, a long white sandy beach on the Pacific Ocean. Here, I will be using the Blessings Chimes and the Vortexes. On this day there is a silver blue hue to the sunlight on the water as dawn appears behind the clouds. An exquisite and beautiful sight. When we arrive, I see the ocean surf is strong, but I am still drawn to walk close to the water's edge.

Before I begin drawing the Vortex Symbols, I bless the ocean waters with the sound of the Blessings Chimes, holding them high up in the air and then down close to the waves. The water responds.

When I begin drawing in the sand close to the water's edge, I note that the water is warm and welcoming. In the distance, over the water a great shaft of Light appears as I am drawing and this shaft stays until all Vortex Symbols are drawn.

The ocean takes the Symbols immediately. A powerful, powerful gift given and received! A miraculous day!

AUM.

In the afternoon, we drive to Point Cartwright, a site overlooking the ocean, to send Didgeridoo music to the Aborigine Spirits in order to thank them for their work with us. We feel their presence but they do not speak.

We have been disappointed not to see or meet any Aborigines living in Australia. Where are they? We have even tried phoning Aborigine companies but no one answers.

May 5:

2:22 a.m., I am up to channel the Aborigines.

An answer comes: *First you have to go out in space and return to find us. We are distant. We are close to the sand and the water and the trees.*

We live between the trees and the rocks and the spaces. Our frequencies are different. Our hearts are the same. We are always at one with Mother Earth, or, at least before the coming of the others. We all need to get in the boat on the water together. There is plenty of space when one is aware. There are times, transition times, when we are close by – the sunrise, the sunset, the earth events – past, present and future. The location of our being is opaque in the cities and suburbs. The music of the Didgeridoo brings us together.

In the morning after breakfast, we want to go to a nearby canal for the healing of the water. We take Baywater Drive to a cluster of eucalyptus and banksia trees by the canal. A black cormorant sits on a post, wings outstretched, drying his wings, seeming to welcome us -- indicating here is where the action is to be.

A white great egret is at the water's edge. Then he flies off and another flies in to check out the scene. This one seems to like us because he stays the entire time of the ceremony – the gifting of the Vortexes Symbols and the ringing of the Blessings Chimes.

Barbara and Stella sit at a picnic table watching me as I begin drawing the Vortex Symbols. Sunlight shines on the Symbols and I feel the Light is very strong when I draw the Universal Law of Symmetry -- as above and so below, heaven on earth, all is in balance.

A bird approaches as I am drawing the Universal Law of Judgment and the Spiritual Law of Karma. He is a young magpie, and his coloring tells me he is six months old. Actually, I feel he is an Aborigine acknowledging what I am doing.

More birds come in, a grey spotted dove and three magpies as I draw the other Vortex Symbols. They feel completely a part of the ceremony. All Nature is one.

As a warbling finale, a bird chorus begins singing in the trees. Stella says this amazing chorus is composed of currawong birds.

Later, in honor of the trees, we search for an ancient forest because we know that early Aborigines slept in tree hollows. They marked these trees and that is why they are called the scarred trees.

Well, we do not find any old trees, but we do stop at a powerful grouping of trees behind a hospital. I give them the sound of the Blessings Chimes and I feel this completes our mission to connect to ancient trees. These trees are telepathic and will deliver the Blessings Chimes message to the ancient trees.

In the late afternoon we drive along the ocean highway near Mount Coolum and here the water feels powerful. I hold the Blessings Chimes to bless the water and the trees.

Tonight I gather my thoughts about this area of the world called Australia. The land is strong and volcanic-based. The ocean and rivers are powerful and embrace the land to help make green fields and trees of all shapes and sizes. The birds nourish themselves from both the land and the water. All are ready to join in ceremony.

I feel joy.

May 6:

Stella drives us early to the Australia Zoo, 28 miles away, because we want to feed the kangaroos. When we reach the zoo, and we are walking to the kangaroo enclosure, we pass two ancient tortoises kissing each other while eating out of the same bowl. Stella's favorite bird, a black-crested cockatoo, calls to her and does a fly-by welcome.

When we reach the kangaroos, we note they are all sizes and colors from light brown to dark. We have special food for them which we put in our palms held flat like a plate.

The kangaroos are not afraid of us. A little one comes up to me and he or she holds onto my hand with both of its hands to make sure to get all the food. This little one is very delicate and very gentle. It is a delight to have this experience.

In another area we see koala bears resting high up in trees. They are so camouflaged, they look like a clump of leaves. Fortunately, some are sleeping in lower trees or on logs so visitors see them up close.

We enjoy watching big emus, relatives of the ostrich, and one walks with us the whole time we are walking along the fence of their large enclosure. How wonderful.

Our next stop is the aviary with amazing birds flying, walking, nesting, sleeping, singing, chirping. To our amazement, some are even swooping over our heads.

Now we go to the Australia Zoo Wildlife Hospital where the public can view through glass a large area for surgery and care for the animals. To show us, a staff member carries to the glass a baby koala bear wrapped in a soft blanket. The little one is holding tight onto his keeper. I look into his eyes and it feels like I am looking into infinity.

We see another koala bear in the hospital and this one is in shock suffering terrible fright from a dog attack. This is an example of why people need to keep their dogs on leashes to avoid this kind of injury. My heart goes out to the animals and to the staff members who so lovingly care for them.

May 9:

I read David Adams' channeled messages that the crystals lines and the Songlines are one, and that the Earth is a new Star within the Cosmos.

I ask the Aborigines, how is this understanding expressed?

Answer: *Enter the door of Love for Mother Earth.*

Where is the door?

Within the heart.

How is the door to be represented?

The grove of trees, the eyes of the koala bear, the song of the birds, the leaps of the dolphins, the light of the dawn, the brilliance of the sunset, the joy of the flowers, the jump of the cats, the Light and Song of the Crystals, the trees, the birds, the flowers, the hearts of humanity. Enter here.

Float above time and place and doing and activity and enter the place of calm -- the Oasis of Calm where details of Life fade away and bliss of being on this magnificent planet permeates the world.

Awaken to this world. Accept through the heart and not the mind. The cells rejoice for they are universal in their being, and even though they are located within a 3D body, they wish to expand and embrace the entire universe.

How does one greet the Aborigines?

Like greeting a sister. The Songlines connect the heart. We are all Earth planetary beings with the same heartbeat. Our Sound and our Light and our Love are the same. Our vessels are different but our essence is the same. We are close to the fine warmth of Mother Earth's heart. We have direct contact because we are not separate from the land and the animals and the birds, all of the Natural World and the Spiritual World. They are all one. You and I are all one. We are together on a magnificent planet with a great capacity for diversification and love. You caught that when you saw the opal reflecting all colors in one crystal.

We reflect all colors, aspects of Mother Earth planet and nature systems upon her and within her. You have stepped into our world. We hear your thoughts and soundings. You come in peace. We greet you in peace. You can find us in that which is not visible and in areas where we are visible.

Australia is our land and others have made it a world land. All must be cherished and honored. Light in the heart opens the way. Come today and give your gift and we shall give ours to you.

I think to myself, Australia is the land where thoughts are heard.

7:07 a.m., we still want to thank the Aborigines for the care of Mother Earth, but we have difficulties reaching them. And so we have decided to make two dozen chocolate chip cookies which we will take to a center called the Nungeena Aboriginal Corporation for Women's Business center at Glass House Mountain.

Stella drives us through high mountains to reach this place and after at least an hour, we turn off the main road to a gravel road that we think will take us to the Aborigine Center.

When we turn off, a house is here and dogs start barking. Then a heavyset man wearing glasses comes out of the house. We tell him we want to give a gift to Aborigines and he comments that Aborigine women will be coming to a meeting called the Elders Council. Perfect, we think! We give him the cookies and he will give them to the Aborigine women. Contact has been made and the gift given. The dogs stop barking and become friendly. Behind the man we see a magnificent mountain and we comment that this mountain is his guardian and he nods yes.

To celebrate success, in the late afternoon when we have returned to Stella's house, I use the Blessings Chimes to honor the Sacred Day and I draw the sacred Vortexes.

May 10:

Stella has another place to show us, the White Eagle Lodge high up in the mountains.*

*See Glossary: White Eagle Lodge, Queensland, Australia.

When we arrive, we are at a center that is exquisitely located in mountains, woods, rose gardens, ferns and other flowers. The meditation room is pure peace.

A meditation is ready to begin, and we are asked if we are interested. Yes.

We enter a room of high-spirited Light and a gentle woman leads the meditation, which is all about Light. Light to the world. Light for healing,

After the meditation, Barbara and I sit in a beautiful rose garden and White Eagle channels to us.

Here is a beacon of peace where people come to be refreshed. The soul center of peace and comfort where truth and love is spoken and received and sent out to the world. Powerful Light. Peace and Harmony and Light. All united.

With love, White Eagle

We return to Twin Waters filled with joy for having this experience at such an amazing place. A place of Peace.

Tomorrow we will say goodbye to Australia and fly to Japan. Australia, we will miss you.

––––––––––––––––––––

May 11:

A shuttle picks us up from Stella's house and delivers us to Brisbane International Airport where we take Qantas Airlines to Narita. During the flight, we realize we are taking Songlines from Australia to Japan.

––––––––––––––––––––

Chapter 5

Japan

From Barbara:

When we arrive at Narita, Japan, we disembark and proceed through Customs for a stamping of our passports and a quick review of required entry paperwork. Then we need to find a free shuttle to take us to the Hilton Hotel at Narita where we will spend the night before going to Tokyo.

Finding the shuttle is easy enough and it is soon proceeding slowly with other shuttles leaving the airport. I am looking out the window at many buildings and I am surprised. Several years ago when I looked out the window there were far fewer buildings. This place Narita I am now looking at is BUSY.

The Hilton Hotel is easy enough to find. A big sign at the top of a towering building announces its name, and the bus driver is soon stopping at the front door to let out passengers. Margaret and I are given comfortable accommodations and we are ready to end the day. Tired!

May 12:

This morning it is easy enough to take a shuttle back to the airport and here we soon find a bus that will take us directly to the Shinagawa Prince Hotel in Tokyo. We will stay two nights and then we will go into the Japanese countryside to stay with a musician friend who is restoring an ancient farmhouse. He already lives there and is composing music from influences around him -- birds, trees, rustic nature.

But just now the focus for Margaret and me is the Tokyo hotel called the Shinagawa Prince Hotel. It is BIG. Actually, it is a complex of several hotel buildings. Our accommodations are in the part called the Main Tower.

Last night, when the shuttle bus driver unloaded our bags and we dragged them into the hotel, we discovered just how big this place is! We also discovered that this hotel complex is an attraction for those ready to be married. To us, this makes sense because marriage guests from all over can gather and stay in this big hotel.

We do notice that places to sit in the lobby area are discouraged because of the lack of chairs and couches except where marriage guests gather to be with each other.

Interesting, we notice that most women in these marriage gatherings are wearing traditional dress not often seen in the streets. They are wearing kimonos with yukatas on their backs.

Just now I have been investigating the Internet for words to explain to you what I saw. In any case, the hotel complex was full of marriage-orientated people.

In the morning, Margaret and I follow signs to reach a hotel aquarium. We want to see dolphins, and yes, we do find the aquarium after wandering around a bit, but it is closed.

Now we understand that the main intent for having the aquarium at the hotel is to have daily shows of dolphins performing in a spectacular manner. This reminds us of when we watched dolphins in Hawaii being trained for a show, and we felt sorry for the dolphins. In Hawaii, the great sea was only yards from them but they had been trapped and brought to the training place to learn tricks. We felt these dolphins would never be free again, and this saddened us. Now we realize that the Tokyo hotel entertainment program includes trapped dolphins who would never be free. And so we do not return to the aquarium to see the dolphins perform.

On May 13, we have been invited to attend a dinner reception at the International House of Japan which is not far from the hotel and so we take a taxi to reach the place. On arrival, we see it is similar to the International House in New York City, a wonderful place to stay and meet people from across the world.

Because we are early for the dinner reception at the International House of Japan, we sit and wait in comfortable chairs close to the main reception desk. Then, suddenly an elevator door opens near us to exit Masami Saionji, chairperson of The World Peace Prayer Society and directress of the dinner reception. This is a wonderful surprise! We fall into each other's arms hugging and kissing. We have known each other a long time and when we meet, it is always unexpected. The cover of one of our earlier books has the three of us together when we are at The Hague in Holland.

Recently, Mrs. Saionji has taken up the work of bringing a better equality between the male and the female, and this work is the main focus of her meeting today at the International House. Margaret and I attend the dinner after the meeting and at the dinner we are delighted to meet people we have met earlier in other parts of the world.

After the dinner party with Masami Saionji and the other invited guests, a new adventure awaits Margaret and me. We will be joining musician Hiro Kawagishi who has invited us to stay at his country home. He will be driving to Tokyo and meet us at the International House. When he arrives, we are speaking with musician James Twyman and within minutes there is an agreement between them. Twyman will be giving a concert in Tokyo in two days and he has brought with him only a banjo. Hiro has a guitar he will loan Twyman, and Hiro, who has a handmade unusual African-style instrument, will become part of Twyman's peace concert! We will attend.

The evening is coming on strongly and Hiro begins driving us to his house. Margaret is in the front seat and I am in the back seat, which I prefer because I don't want to see cars coming toward us 'on the wrong side of the road'. Will I ever adjust to this 'other side of the road' custom which is so different from the 'American side of the road'?

In any case, Hiro confidently drives us to his home, about two hours, and I am looking out the side window at the city of Tokyo, waiting for the countryside. Japan feels so packed with people, it hardly seems possible that there will be a countryside with only a few buildings. Well, yes, this scenery does arrive and I look at it with curiosity.

When we do arrive at Hiro's house, it is completely dark. He stops his car in front of his house, and with a flashlight, he helps us walk a few feet to sit on concrete steps. Here, we take off our shoes, as is the custom when entering a Japanese home, and we put on slippers offered by Hiro.

The inside of the house has lights, which he turns on, and we are led to a bedroom to spend the night. Slippers are waiting for us as we reach the bedroom doorway, and we put them on before sleeping in a traditional Japanese bedroom of blankets on the floor.

What fun! And, how comfortable!

In the morning Hiro treats us to a delicious Japanese breakfast, and we begin this meal by eating bamboo, which is DELICIOUS. He tells us that this bamboo comes from trees once growing behind the house. After breakfast, he takes us outside to tour the grounds. We begin walking only a few steps when he stops, reaches down, pulls up the top of something growing, and hands it to us to eat. An herb, he explains as we eat.

When we reach the corner of the house, he follows the side of the house to the back where a lone, big tree is growing. This is bamboo, he says, and then he explains that he has spent hours and hours cutting down bamboo trees growing behind the house because they were infringing on the house.

I tell him that the lone bamboo tree misses his brothers and sisters, and he understands and says the tree looks sad. I suggest that maybe he can plant some flowers near the sad tree as company.

In any case, it is fun walking outside the house, and the feeling of the countryside is strong.

Now Hiro is ready to take us to the water where we will give Love to the water. Interesting, I use the word 'Pacific' but Margaret uses another word, although we are in agreement as to the work.

Hiro puts us in his car for a drive to the water and just as we are beginning the drive, he says we must first visit a nearby shrine.

Yes! Of course. Yes!

He drives us less than three minutes and then makes a sharp turn to drive between rice fields sending up their bounty for humanity. I realize that if we stop between these rice fields to get out of the car, we would be standing in one of these rice fields.

Well, we did not stop and when we reach the end of the rice fields, we are at an ancient shrine. It is a simple shrine, but one can feel the power of this place.

We leave the car and I walk to a very old tree growing straight up at the shrine's entrance. I call this a talking tree that records all that occurs here, and I pat the tree and say hello.

He reminds me of the 700-year-old tree far south of here that I petted several years ago when we, including Hiro, were with a Japanese monk.

Now we begin driving again to the water. Hiro says he knows how to reach the water but he has never stopped. He is driving only a short time before we see the water and he parks his car and we walk to it. This is not a long stretch of coastline. It is a small water inlet sitting between rustic nature, and this inlet ends near us in the form of a small, sandy beach.

Yes, we are at the Pacific. One does not have to see the entire ocean to know what one is looking at.

Margaret, with Vortexes in her hands and tiny, crystalline chimes, walks to the edge of the water and Hiro and I stand a bit further back. We three are ready in our own way to energize the water. Hiro has in his hands a kora which he has made himself, a replica of an ancient African musical instrument like a harp. I stand beside him holding a big piece of a bamboo tree. The ends are sealed, and when I turn the bamboo up-side-down, I hear tiny noises indicating that what is in there is trickling down. When the trickling noise stops, I turn the bamboo the other way, and tiny noises begin again.

There is life here, wood speaking, participating, during the ceremony of honoring and giving energy to help heal the water. All have a consciousness. All can participate.

The wind knows. It begins blowing powerfully.

One time, about ten years ago, when Margaret and I were standing on the Great Wall of China, we blew healing energy around the world via the Great Wall. We sent it out to the East and it returned from the West. Now, at the water, the wind cooperates with us by blowing healing energy around the world.

However, a problem begins. A man, wife and small child come to the tiny beach to paddle their boat. They bring it as a wrapped thin plastic sheet which they begin to straighten out as a boat. But, the wind is so strong, this thin plastic sheet suddenly and violently throws itself up in the air and across the beach.

The man and woman run to catch it, make it into a boat, and take it to the water. When the man puts it in the water, he tells the little girl to get into the head of the boat, but she refuses. She is afraid. He INSISTS. And so, with the wind blowing powerfully, she tumbles into the boat and nearly falls into the water. The strength of the wind is so great, we know that if she had tumbled into the water, she probably would have drowned. Now the man gets into the boat and struggles hard to paddle it out to sea, but the wind is too strong.

Just at this moment, we finish our healing work and the wind stops! All is calm and the man begins effortlessly to paddle his boat. The crisis is over.

This was an example of humans not foreseeing what they should have been foreseeing. They wanted so much to paddle their boat, they were violating common sense. The wind was too powerful for a safe journey. Death was ready to interfere.

A few years earlier, we were at a seaside beach when powerful waves were coming in. A man was having fun thrashing around in the mighty waves, ignoring the strength of them. Then he suddenly stopped moving. A heart attack killed him.

Interesting, in Japan we are doing ocean healing when the experience of near death became foreseeable.

Healing and death are opposite experiences. The healing won.

We ask Hiro to return us to the shrine, the holy place, and he has immediately agreed. Here, I go to the big recording tree, pat him, and give him a mental recording of what had just happened at the beach regarding healing and the opposite,,,,near death.

When it is time to attend a yearly event called Symphony of Peace Prayers (SOPP), Hiro drives us to its location at the foot of sacred

Mount Fuji. Thousands from across the world will gather here to participate in acts of prayer and harmony for the world.

This will be the twelfth such event. Last year, the SOPP focused on a global initiative called The Fuji Declaration which asked all of us to awaken our Divine Spark to help with the creation of a more peaceful civilization on Mother Earth. A song was sung. We Are All Shining Divine Sparks, and it will be sung again this year.

A new concept to be introduced this year is called the Soul Of WoMen. Its motive is to help balance society by balancing male and female characteristics because it is believed that this will help release uneven concepts and embrace balance and equality on the planet.

Attending will be religious leaders of different faiths to give their prayers for peace, and the audience will join in. Again, the motive is to bring balance and harmony throughout the world.

I know there will be those in the audience whom I have met over the years, and so the event will feel like a grand reunion. Yes, for me, this will be an enjoyable moment at the foot of sacred Mount Fuji.

And so, I am sitting again in the back seat of Hiro's car while he is driving us northward to the sanctuary at Mount Fuji. It is a long drive, but we move along steadily until we are about ten miles from our destination. Then, traffic begins slowing us to a crawl. I know there will be many attending today's SOPP event.

Unexpectedly, Hiro makes an abrupt left turn away from the main highway. He says he knows a short cut and he drives into a forest rich with trees. We move along steadily with no cars in front of us or behind us, and quite quickly we come to the area of the sanctuary headquarters. Here, we meet many, many cars, and uniformed security men are waving drivers here and there to park in assigned lots.

But, Hiro continues toward the main entrance because he knows Margaret and I, as honored guests of today's event, must be registered and then taken to special seating. Hiro, with his car idling, opens the door, gets out, and tells us he will search on foot for where we should register.

Well, he is less than two minutes gone when uniformed Security are at the car talking to us in Japanese. We smile and speak in English that we do not understand Japanese.

And so, there is a dilemma. How is it to be solved? Security has an answer. They motion with their arms that the car must move and they can move it. Is that all right with us?

Yes, yes, of course.

And so, one security man gets into the idling car and moves it about fifteen feet and stops. He is satisfied the car will not obstruct traffic.

When Hiro returns to see that the car has been moved, he asks who moved it. "The police," we answer with a smile, and he is shocked! Never mind, we tell him with another smile. No harm done.

Well, now we go to the place for the registering of honored guests, and here Margaret and I not only are given a sign to wear with our names on it, but we are also given a gorgeous white rose. Instantly, I am sad because I know we will not be allowed to fly overseas with flowers. However, when I touch the rose, I realize it is artificial. Hurray! It will go home with me.

A young, female attendant speaking excellent English begins taking charge, and soon we are seated in an honored guest section. I am seated next to a distinguished young man, an Iraqi, and Margaret is seated next to a Turkish couple wearing distinguished Turkish clothes. The husband is a Muslim cleric.

We are all seated on open benches and the weather is perfect with a bright blue sky and sunshine. In front of me is a woman wearing a wide, wide straw hat and enough wind blows so that her hat flies off and drops behind her, just in front of me. I pick it up and return it to her. She takes it with a smile and then she reaches for a similar hat on her lap and gives it to me.

THANK YOU!

Over the course of the SOPP program, her hat falls off three times and I return it to her. Mine stays seated, and at the end of the program, I return it to her. Yes, I have thoughts of keeping it, but it really is not mine. I note that when I return the hat to her, she is relieved. Obviously she thought I would be keeping it, but she probably had other plans for it.

Before the program is over, the name of each honored guest is announced and we, as expected, rise and bow Japanese style to the audience.

I note that James Twyman has been asked to play his banjo for the audience, and he plays wonderful peace music. The audience applauds enthusiastically.

The last event of the program is for the honored guests to attend a reception where food is offered. I am seated next to an older Muslim with a red beard. He speaks English and we soon are speaking. He tells me he lives in Japan and he is of Pakistani origin. Now, that is interesting. I tell him the contents of an email received just before I left the USA to come to Australia and Japan. A Pakistani friend, a lawyer living in Pakistan, has been helping a poor girl about six years old who was born with a cleft pallet. Her parents had no money to repair her mouth, but when my friend learned about the young girl's plight, he managed to gather enough money. However, the girl cannot speak because she does not know any words to speak. She has a hearing problem.

I give this news to the Muslim male with the red beard and he hands me his name card with an email address. He says the girl's plight should be given to him and this information will be sent to those in Pakistan who are in a position to help the young child.

Wonderful!

One never knows who one will be speaking to. Well, this one I have spoken to may result in success for the girl.

When it is time for say good-bye to SOPP, we are driven to Tokyo by Mitsusu Ooba, a friend who is a photographer. One of his photographs is on the cover of one of our earlier books.

Today is Sunday, and it feels as if all in Japan are driving cars. The pace is slow because of so many drivers, and yet all seem to be patient. There is no honking of horns. Then we learn that 25 kilometers of traffic headed toward Tokyo is stalled. A decision is made to take us to Yokohama and then we will approach Tokyo from that direction.

Well, the traffic continues to be slow, slow, slow, and finally another plan is made for us. We are to take the train, which will be much, much faster.

An English-speaking German woman is with us in the car and she knows the trains well. She will accompany us the full way, to the doorstep of the Shinagawa Prince Hotel where we have reservations for the remainder of our time in Japan.

Yes, everything works out very well. We are taken to the train station and the German woman helps us buy tickets for the right trains (we use two trains). Then she stays with us until we enter the hotel in Tokyo.

WOW!!!

WONDERFUL.

Our hotel accommodations on the 31st floor look out at miles and miles and miles of faceless skyscrapers -- mostly the color of light or dark grey. We are too far above the ground to see roads or cars or people. At one place, we can see the tops of a few trees.

I do not feel humanity within this great city of over 13 million people. Is anyone living here? Is anyone working here?

In the evening when the sun goes down and the sky is dark, lights begin to appear in the faceless buildings. Then there are more lights and more lights and more lights. Yes, now there is evidence of humanity in this gigantic, faceless place.

We have just learned that Sydney, Australia, puts on a magnificent show by lighting up its buildings with brilliant colors, especially its opera house. If Tokyo lighted up its city with brilliant colors, think how impressive this would be!

Yes, Tokyo needs to color itself.

We feel an earthquake. Not a large one, but, nevertheless, an earthquake. We know that attention has been given to a possibility of earthquakes when these buildings were constructed, but, how can anyone know what would happen if a very big earthquake suddenly occurred? Could we get away? Using elevators probably would be 'off limits'.

Yes, we have thoughts about the earthquake, but there is little we can do, and so we carry on as if nothing has happened.

Now it is time to concentrate on our last event in Japan. We have been invited to James Twyman's peace concert at a place in central Tokyo called the Akasaka Civic Center.

How are we to reach this place? There is no one to take us. The train is the only way. Taking a taxi would cost a fortune.

When it is time to begin this adventure, we have in our hands a map to show various lines, and we cross the hotel road to the train station. We quickly board a train taking us to a station stop where we are to get out and take another line.

Well, we do not know this, but we are ready to run into a problem. When we reach the transfer station and get out, we expect to see some signs in English to direct us. No signs. We walk a bit along the platform looking for some indication of where we should go, but we can understand nothing. There are plenty of people on the platform.

The place is packed with them. All Japanese. A station director standing nearby may be the answer.

No. He speaks no English. And so we walk a bit more, but when we reach stairs taking us either up or down, we do not know what to do. We stop and I say to Margaret, "We need to ask the Higher Worlds for HELP."

We do this and in less than a minute, a man in front of us turns and asks in clear English, "Do you need help?"

YES.

Where are you from, we ask him. SYDNEY, AUSTRALIA is the answer.

Amazing!!!!

We tell him where we want to go and he explains in easy terms that we cannot take the train. We must walk upstairs and take the subway. And so we do this, and we have no problems.

When we reach the station close to the Akasaka Civic Center, we leave the subway and exit to a city street where there is a big hotel. A uniformed hotel woman is standing at the entrance and we ask her in English if she would wave down a taxi that would take us to nearby Akasaka Civic Center.

Yes!

Soon a taxi is whisking us to the Center and we are there within minutes. As we enter the place, we are directed to take an elevator to the James Twyman concert which is about to begin. In fact, we arrive just ten minutes before it begins.

About a dozen of our friends, mostly American, are there, and they ask how we arrived. When we tell them we have taken the train and subway, they NEARLY FAINT. They would NEVER do this, they tell us.

Well, we did, and we succeeded, but I doubt if we will ever do that again!

There are many at the concert we are happy to be with. We greet Mrs. Saionji, and we hug James Twyman and Hiro. And yes, the concert is WONDERFUL. The music is WONDERFUL.

Afterward, we are invited to join a taxi of people returning to the Shinagawa Prince Hotel area for dinner, and when we arrive, we eat with about twenty people who have attended the concert. This is a very busy restaurant with a large selection of food.

Today, May 19, 5 p.m., we end our Japan journey when we board a plane at Narita Airport to fly nonstop to Newark, New Jersey, arriving 4:55 p.m., May 19, the same date! Well, if we had left Japan the evening of April 28 after I had had a full day in Japan on my birthday, then, in theory, we would be having April 28 the entire journey to Newark, New Jersey, in the eastern part of the U.S.A.

That would have made a VERY LONG birthday for me!

CHAPTER 6

JAPAN

From Margaret:

April 25:

Sakurajima is the most active volcano in Japan. His job is to remove excess energy from the interior of Mother Earth by exploding excess energy. He knows Barbara and me, and one time he blew us a little heart cloud when we physically visited him. He has given both of us messages written in ancient calligraphy which we have had translated.

Recently there has been an increase of earthquakes in Japan. I channel Sakurajima asking for suggestions on how to stabilize the country. What can we do to help, I ask him. Where should we put our focus?

Sakurajima answers: *Your focus reflects your frequency. When approaching the guardians of the plates and plate boundaries, announce your arrival with the frequency of peace and tranquility, not fear or being on alert.*

In Japan, you will be walking into a high-spirited land, and like horses, the earth can respond with a quick jolt. Address the guardians of the plates, the elementals. Ask for stability. Ask for plate movement in a smooth fashion and not in abrupt quakes.

Hold your focus. Steady your frequency. Eyes and ears and heart turned toward the beauty of the land. Bless the land, the water, the air, the fire beneath. Find stability within yourself so you can send that frequency to Mother Earth and her elements.

Humanity needs to bring frequency into balance and love. Barriers come down with love and peace frequency. Let the musicians play a soft beautiful song for harmony and balance and peace. A wonderful gathering in the coming weeks. Hearts open. Frequency focus steady. Balance.

Greetings from an old friend, Sakurajima.

Now it is May 12, and Barbara and I are in Japan relaxing in a quiet room at Hilton Tokyo Narita Airport Hotel. Yesterday we arrived in Japan from Australia. I am sitting in a beam of light coming from a small opening of the curtains. This light is welcoming the morning. I say, good morning, Sun. Good morning, Japan. So good to return to your beautiful land.

I have brought with me the Blessings Chimes from Australia to give to Japan Love, Peace, Healing, Harmony and Balance. May Peace Prevail on Earth.

I have also brought with me the energy of Songlines. Barbara and I know Songlines follow the heart lines.

I receive this channeling:

Songlines are Light lines, energy lines, merging with crystalline energy grid lines. Love frequencies dial up the energy frequencies of the systems that have merged. Humans can turn their attention to the being-ness of the Songlines, the heart lines of Mother Earth.

In a vision in Australia, you saw a diagram of the conjunction of the Songlines in the form of ancient brick archways meeting and intersecting in a 3D way – moving, joining, separating and continuing on. Blessed be the Songlines that envelop the world.

The Blessings Chimes you bring with you awaken and cheer on the connection of humans to Songlines energies wherever you are. It is like a bird song awakening the plants to grow and rejoice in the Sun's powerful light of Love and nutrients and growth. Peace, Peace, Peace. The ancient bells come forth to sew the dimensions, to reach out to the root systems of Light.

AUM

As the sun is pouring into the room, I place the Blessings Chimes and the Vortexes on a circular table. I open the curtains wide to see the sky and clouds that look like a dove, a dragon and four dolphins around a heart. Amazing! I remember Sakurajima's heart cloud. I am seeing clouds as spaceships. The day is fresh and bright and expanding.

When it is time, we make our way to Tokyo to stay at the Shinagawa Prince Hotel, which is vast, complex, and somewhat impersonal. Everyone is busy, busy, busy. Many Japanese, both men and women, are wearing formal black and white business garb.

We are assigned to a room on Floor 26 which gives us a view of the city. The bright sun is blazing in as we put out the Vortexes and I ring the Blessings Chimes for Tokyo. Later, I ring them again for sacred Mount Fuji which is now visible in the distance. What a delight!!!

May 13:

I am looking out the window at a cloudy, overcast morning. The city below has the colors of whites, greys, and brown. When we take the elevator to the lobby, we see a number of wedding parties. Men are wearing formal dress and women are wearing traditional silk kimonos. Photographs are being taken. Everyone is waiting for weddings. Because the hotel is so huge, I understand why everyone is assembled here in the lobby waiting for weddings.

Our main focus today is an event called the Soul of WoMen International Gathering.* The purpose of the gathering is to discuss the need for a joining of the Divine Feminine with the Divine Masculine to bring balance and harmony to society so that peace will flourish in the world. We will be at the gathering at dinnertime when we have been asked to say a few words.

*See Glossary: Soul of WoMen International Gathering, Tokyo, May 13.

Today's event will be at the International House of Japan, and when we arrive we meet Mrs. Masami Saionji, head of the World Peace Prayer Society and organizer of this event. She is happy to see us and we embrace her as she gives us a dear welcome. Soon we are meeting long-time friends of the World Peace Prayer Society and we are introduced to others from around the world. When it is our turn to talk, we speak briefly about our world work to bring balance and harmony.

At the event, we meet peace troubadour James Twyman who will be giving a peace concert in Tokyo in a couple days. We will attend. And now another musician comes, Hiro Kawagishi, who has invited us to his farmhouse. We met him several years ago at a conference in Istanbul and since then we have been regularly in touch with him by email. Now he has driven to Tokyo to take us to his farmhouse.

When it is time to leave with him, we begin a two-hour amazing drive through interesting sections of Tokyo, then a complex expressway through tunnels including the long one under the Bay of Tokyo. We arrive at his old farmhouse which introduces us to the traditional Japanese way of living -- tatami mats, sliding doors, sunken cooking area in a central room, mat and futons on the floor as beds. The kitchen and bathroom are modern. We LOVE this place!

May 14:

In the early morning, I walk outside to listen to birds singing in the trees. Some trees are bamboo. I know bird singing makes the grass, garden and herbs grow. Later, when we are all up, we walk outside to see happy trees, happy land. Orange trees send out fragrant smells. Frogs are singing in nearby rice fields.

Hiro cooks breakfast for us and this includes bamboo. We have never tasted bamboo or even conceived that it is cooked. Yes, we love eating it, plus the fennel tea.

Margaret Channeling: A message from the trees.

We welcome you here to this land. We hold stable the influence of the changing seasons and times. The birds are our allies and dance among our leaves and make their homes in our branches. We hold and send peace to the land. We send the light to Mother Earth. We are her hair. We express her love. We receive and give love. We are healers. We dance with the wind. We move with communications of all. We have our own Songlines, energy.

The bamboo shoots, they are a part of our forest. We welcome you. We give you our blessings and we will receive blessings from you. You move. We stand. When you stand and see and feel, you are a part of us. Enjoy the bright sun. Enjoy the day of Peace. Every day is a day of peace when there is no disturbance among the trees. Peace be with you and go with you. We hold the heart line of the land.

The trees of the land.

Here is channeling from the Guardian of the Land and the Songlines:

Where are the Songlines? In the earth? Carried by the wind? Engraved in the rocks? All of the above. The Songlines come down from above and enter the land frequency via the trees, via the water (falls, streams, and oceans), via those that carry the receptors to hear, feel, carry the Songlines frequency. Songlines move. Songlines are timeless. Songlines are continuous flowing energy enlivening the beautiful Planet of Earth.

This planet is a vast garden and we are the energy tubes, paths, currents. Yes, all enliven the Earth systems. To think too hard on the Songlines makes us become dim. The mind interferes. Let the energy flourish. You cannot stop the winds and the water movement nor can you change or stop the lines. We have our own force field and guardian systems.

Flow with us. Dip into our currents. We are continuous. Love frequency opens the door to the frequencies of life force, electrical systems, energy lines, music lines, color lines, crystal lines, fragrance lines. The orange, the jasmine, the herbs, the soil all carry the nurturing components of the Songlines. The lines are straight; the lines are curving; the lines are single; the lines are complex and branching. Watch the flow of energy — up and down, within and without, under and away, all around. Profound.

The Guardian of the Land and the Songlines.

———————————

After breakfast, it is time to go to the Pacific Ocean to sound the Blessings Chimes for the healing of the waters. Hiro wants to take us first to an ancient nearby shrine. To approach the shrine we need to drive between rice fields that are growing just inches from an ancient wall wide enough for carriages. We drive on this wall.

When we reach the base of the shrine, we park the car and climb the stairs to greet guardian trees and the Spirits of the shrine. The shrine is over 300 years old and, according to tradition, had been moved to this place.

We ring the ancient bell by pulling a long rope to wake up the Spirits of the sacred shrine above the rice fields. A great white heron flies by in greeting. We pray for the land of Japan and for the oceans. Now we drive out of the rice fields and into a river-forest area that has the feeling of wild deer living here. Earlier, Hiro has spotted a great antlered male deer here.

We are now on the coastline and driving to Ubara Beach to give the Vortexes and sound the Blessings Chimes for the healing of the water. We know the Pacific is in great peril because of the Fukushima accident that has affected all life forms in the ocean. We want to go immediately to the ocean to give healing, and now we are here.

For me, Ubara is a special beach. It has many layered rock formations and a natural bridge has been carved out by the ocean. I am ready to draw the Vortexes Symbols. The surf is low as I kneel at the water's edge to draw them. When I draw, I speak to the water to say that the energy put down is for the world's oceans and especially the ocean area suffering from the damage of Fukushima. In all, I draw twenty-two Symbols, one beside the other, along the beach at the water's edge. Each is encircled for activation. Very important are the Symbols of Universal Law of Innocence, Truth and Family and Spiritual Protection of Family. This pertains to all life forms in the ocean.

As I am drawing, I reach a piece of sea grass laying at the exact spot where the next Symbol is to go. What is the Symbol? Universal Law of Change! It is the lower part of the Symbol! I include the sea grass as I draw the Symbol. This Symbol indicates what is needed now – CHANGE.

After all the Symbols are drawn, great winds blow the Vortex energy around the world. Before I began drawing the Symbols, the wind was relatively calm, but when I started drawing, it picked up and became very powerful.

I see flying above me in the distance a black hawk and a black crow. Then, far above them, I see a bald eagle flying and later a golden eagle.

Barbara and Hiro have been accompanying my drawing of the Symbols. Hiro plays the kora, an ancient African instrument, and

Barbara plays the rain stick, a bamboo piece that originated from Hiro's backyard. The two give the music to the ocean for harmony and healing.

It is 12 noon and the wind continues blowing at gale force, sending the energy out around the world. Now I am playing the Blessings Chimes for the waters of the Pacific.

While this is happening, there is drama on the beach within a few feet of us. A father and a daughter are attempting to put an inflatable boat in the rough water with the high winds. They want to paddle. We know that paddling now would be very dangerous but they do not stop their attempts. Fortunately, after we finish the music-sound-healing for the oceans, the wind stops. The people are spared.

We return to the ancient shrine and report the event to the great trees that will record the message and send the message out to the trees of the entire world.

Now I stop for a moment to admire a beautiful butterfly perched on the wall of the shrine. The butterfly is Guardian of the Universal Law of Change. I feel I am in PARADISE. I love the ancient shrine. I love the trees. I love the ancient farmhouse.

In the evening, we listen to Hiro playing the kora for us. It is magic. He tells us that while driving his car, in his mind he receives music in phrases. Immediately he calls his cell phone and sings the melody. When he reaches his home, he puts the phrases together and records them.

I receive a channeling that Hiro's music is *Song Lines of Universal Harmonies.*

May 15:

Very early this morning we begin a lengthy drive to Mount Fuji to attend the SOPP, the Symphony of Peace Prayers.* Barbara and I are invited as guests of honor and we are given white rose badges. We are seated with dignitaries facing a large stage.

*See Glossary: Symphony of Peace Prayers.

The May 15 SOPP is an outdoor event near sacred Mount Fuji. Many have come from around the world to attend this annual event which concentrates on bringing people together in peace. Mrs. Saionji is on stage to give a powerful speech for peace, balance and harmony on the planet.

Religious dignitaries are invited to speak their prayers for peace and the entire audience repeats these prayers. Then there is an emotional Flag Ceremony where flags are presented for each country as well as peace prayers for each. Many in the audience have tears.

During the ceremony is a musical performance of James Twyman who sings May Peace Prevail On Earth and We are All Shining Divine Sparks. He lights the stage with his love for peace and admiration for the work of the World Peace Prayer Society. 10,000 people attend the SOPP ceremony. Afterward, when we guests of honor walk to a reception, Mount Fuji comes out in all its glory! What a splendid moment!

Margaret Channeling from the Sun:

From Fuji comes the frequency of Peace held within the structure of the mountain and by the many prayers of the World Peace Prayer Society gathering. Their prayers lay like lace over Nature – nurturing the surroundings and the world. The waters wait for the light for clarity. The wind, the fire, the land, the water are all nurtured by me.

My blessing this afternoon, dear one. The Sun.

Mount Fuji comes in:

Blessings to the Japanese people who work hard and are devoted to peace. That is why my presence was visible at the end of the SOPP celebration. I came to bless the occasion.

The Sun speaks again:

Now we will soon share the holy hour of the sunset. The light changes. The earth changes to receive the night – the absence of my light except for the moon which reflects my light. Systems shut down without my light.

That is why my light looks/feels so brilliant now at the time of 5:00 p.m. The painters knew this time – the light intensity is different and richer.

Rest in the blessing light.

With my love, the Sun. My love to your beloved planet Earth.

Mount Fuji speaks again:

The people gathered at my base and the air was sweet and the sun bright with a sweet breeze blowing. The people gathered as the birds gather at my base. Harmony prevailed. Everyone had the same thought form, Peace. May Peace Prevail On Earth. All the colors of the flags were woven into one. There was no division and separation. There was unity of purpose. The frequency of peace is lighter than the frequency of conflict. Thus the Peace Vibration floated up to me in my heights. Vibration. I broadcast the peace outwards.

CHAPTER 7

ARKANSAS

From Barbara:

I need to give you background on why Margaret and I go to the state of Arkansas in June before the Solstice. This place on the North American continent was the major growing field for crystals during the time before the destruction of Atlantis a long time ago.

When it was realized that Atlantis would be destroyed, three major crystals residing in Atlantis were sent inter-dimensionally to Arkansas and were put to sleep. Now they are awake. We visit Arkansas to familiarize ourselves with these crystals.

But before we put our complete attention on the crystals, we must first put our attention on Pinnacle Mountain in Arkansas where the energy of the three awakened crystals can be directed.

What is Pinnacle Mountain? A major Sun Disc that helps distribute energy throughout the world. There are 12 of these major Sun Discs and each is connected to 12 smaller ones. Thus, there are 144 Sun Discs around the world.

Consciously sending the energy of three major crystals to the Pinnacle Mountain Sun Disc means that this Sun Disc will be sending the energy via all 144 Sun Discs to energize the entire world. These crystals are friends for helping to push humanity from the third to the fifth and higher dimensions. It should be noted that they will remain in Arkansas far underground, physically out of reach of humans.

For Margaret and me, within the past ten years it is our third and most important return to Arkansas. On arrival in Little Rock, we will rent a car and drive a few minutes to the Toltec Mounds to give our regards to the Sirian/Pleiadean/Arcturian Command that has been managing the Arkansas show for a great number of years. Then we expect to drive to the Sun Disc Pinnacle Mountain that receives energy from crystals and distributes these energies.

From Pinnacle Mountain we will go to Eureka Springs to give our regards to the Platinum Crystal at Magnetic Mount that resides far underground and is 100 meters high. It has to do with consciousness of the physical and anti-matter (angels), and also it has to do with Christ consciousness that involves cosmic energy humanity should be increasingly using.

From Eureka Springs we will go to Mount Magazine, site of the Emerald Crystal, which has to do with the energy of the heart and healing. This crystal is 20 meters high and 5 meters wide.

From there we go to Talimena Ridge where there is the Blue Crystal of Knowledge, 48 feet high and 12 feet wide.

From Talimena Ridge we may go to two mines open to the public, and we do not expect to do anything except look briefly at these mines. Then we go to Mount Ida and this place has huge numbers of crystals. We expect to overnight at nearby Lake Ouachita because this lake has to do with Christ cosmic energies.

On our list of visits is the diamond area where people can pick up diamonds that are relatively easy to find at a plowed field. From there, probably we may stop for a moment or two at a place called Magnet Cove to acknowledge the energy here that is such that a compass cannot function properly if it is used to find directions.

After we do all this, we will fly from Arkansas to New York City to participate in the Paul Winter Summer Solstice event. Here, we will witness a cosmic door opening to send energy to our world. The Sun Discs, including Pinnacle Mountain, as well as the three major awakened Atlantean crystals, will be significant players for distributing this energy. And, there is more. When a door is opened, energy can go both ways -- to our world and from our world. At the Solstice we will be sending peace energy out the door to other worlds. That will be our world contribution. Peace energy.

May Peace Prevail on Earth and everywhere.

Now that the background for this chapter is explained, I will begin telling you about our journey to Arkansas.

June 10, Joan, our faithful taxi driver, takes us to the airport to catch a flight to Chicago's airport, followed by a flight to Little Rock. Our first pilot takes us above clouds, and when he is ready to reach the Chicago airport, he dips below them and we soon arrive. When we touch the plane windows, we know that Chicago is hot, but we already know this. We also know that Little Rock will probably be even hotter. Never mind. Our attention is on the three Atlantean crystals, not the weather.

When we reach Little Rock, yes, it is hot. Very hot. Without looking at a weather gauge, my estimate is that the thermometer is hovering around 100 degrees Fahrenheit.

At the airport, we are directed to rental cars, and Hertz rents us a small black car that we soon discover is completely NEW. An attendant shows us car factors that need to be learned before we can begin our journey. But, we did not check how to use the windshield wipers, and on the second day, when it started to rain, we had a problem. The on-and-off knob will not automatically work! A hand needs to dwell constantly on the knob to turn the wipers on or off.

OH!!!!

Well, this unwelcome factor ends when we stop at a gas station to ask for help. A man sticks his arm through the open window, hits the knob with a mighty THUD and the knob sinks. The wipers begin behaving obediently.

Yes, I think we are the first customers to drive this completely new car!

Well, the first day of our journey, when there is no perceived rain or windshield wiper problem, we head toward the Toltec Mounds to announce our arrival to the Sirian/Pleiadean/Arcturian Command that has been functioning here for thousands of years. We have our maps with us and we drive along confidently because we have earlier visited this place.

But, after a time, because we see no signs to the Toltec Mounds, we begin wondering if something is wrong. Are we on the right road? We turn around to head toward the airport, and before we arrive, we take another road which still does not give us confidence.

The area is thinly populated, but we see a small building set a bit back from the road, and this small building has a big sign -- LIQUOR. A customer is leaving the building with something in his hands, and before he can get into his car, we drive up, stop, roll down our window and ask him if he knows the location of the Toltec Mounds.

YES!

He says when he drives to and from his house, he is always passing a sign to the mounds. We should drive just behind him and he will show us the sign.

And so our small black car begins following his small white car. He drives somewhat slowly and we feel he is thinking we probably drive slower than he does.

Well, sure enough. We come to a big roadside sign announcing the location of the Toltec Mounds. He slows and we blink on and off our headlights as a way of thanking him for his kindness.

When we drive into the parking lot, we are surprised to see that it is nearly empty. Maybe the temperature intent on breaking heat records has discouraged anyone from coming. We park and enter the Visitor's Center and say hello to the only person inside the place, the director. We speak with him a moment or two before he asks if we wish to see a short video of the mounds.

Yes.

He nods his head in the direction of the next room and we enter to take two seats of one hundred or more available. The room lights are turned off and the video begins.

Does it give us an explanation of the command post beneath the Toltec Mounds? No, and this is understandable. The commend post is not in the third dimension. The video does explain that years ago many mounds were built on this continent but little is known about who built them and why they were built except probably many were ceremonial sites.

Ceremonial sites? Why?

We do learn that an examination has shown that some mounds were built according to the position of the sun at the solstices and equinoxes. Archeologists are continuing to study them.

Well, Margaret and I have come to the Toltec Mounds to acknowledge to the Sirian/Pleiadean/Arcturian Command our presence in Arkansas, site of the Atlantean crystals. We are satisfied. We have given our greetings and now it is time for us to go to the Embassy Suites Hotel where we have reservations.

We drive our little black car toward the Little Rock Airport, officially called the Bill and Hillary Clinton National Airport, to hook onto an express route called West 440. This, we know, will have much traffic, but it is a good road with many lanes, and so the traffic will move relatively quickly.

And yes, it does move fast and the next roads we take are fast. The hotel is not close to the airport and so we need to drive quite a while, but we have no difficulty finding it. We cheer when we reach our destination.

The Embassy Suites has a luxury we love -- elevators with backs as windows so one can look down on people leisurely dining on the ground floor. One wants to join them.

Well, we will join them tomorrow morning, but this evening we will be eating across the street at the Kobe Restaurant that serves first-class, affordable Japanese food. We ate here when we stayed at the Embassy Suites during our last visit to Arkansas. I remember ending my meal with a bowl of vanilla ice cream and a bit of chocolate sauce. A tiny, colorful Japanese-style umbrella was perched on the ice cream. I want my meal tonight to end the same way, and it does.

After a good night's sleep, we take the elevator down, looking through the windows at people eating breakfast. We see some empty tables and we will use one of them.

This is a buffet type breakfast with one unique offering -- a big omelet made by a chef according to how we eaters want it made. As he cooks the omelet, we stand within a couple feet of him, conversing with him. What fun!

After breakfast, we check out of the hotel to begin a day's work involving the three Atlantean crystals living beneath the land of Arkansas. First we will go to Pinnacle Mountain, the sun disc energy location for the three crystals. The hotel is not far from Pinnacle Mountain, if one does not get lost trying to go there. In 2013, we were very lost when we tried to find the place, but now one should not concentrate on being LOST. Confidence is needed. Today we put faith in our minds and a road map in our hands.

As we begin our journey full of confidence, we go along for a time and then we realize that our map is not telling us to turn left or right or go straight ahead. When we see a big red fire truck in a parking lot with no other vehicles and only one idle man, we drive into the parking lot to ask this man how to reach Pinnacle Mountain. My thought is that if he is connected to the fire truck, he must know where everything within miles is located. He cannot stop by the roadside to consult a map!

And yes, he quickly gives us easy instructions for reaching Pinnacle Mountain. THANK YOU, FIRE MAN.

We soon see Pinnacle Mountain looming near us and very quickly we come to a sign telling us we have reached a recreational area. We turn right to enter and we remember this place from three years ago. A short drive will take us to a waterway which is where earlier Margaret put down Vortexes. Today she stands at the water to send the wonderful energy of the Blessings Chimes to the water.

Paradise. We feel we have reached Paradise.

An eagle flies overhead.

If there is nothing more to do today except be leisurely, we would love to remain here for a time, but we cannot. We should drive to the Pinnacle Mountain Visitor's Center where, three years ago, we had a wonderful chat with the Center's manager. We also saw a baby alligator living by himself in a display case. And, just outside the front door to the Visitor's Center we watched hummingbirds as they noisily flapped their wings while eating food put out for them.

Now we arrive at the Visitor's Center and we learn that the alligator of three years ago has been substituted for another small alligator that is hiding itself behind a log. The hummingbirds are busy somewhere other than the Visitor's Center, and the Center's manager is different from 2013.

Well, one cannot expect everything to remain the same. Our need is to be within the energy field of Pinnacle Mountain which will distribute world wide the energy coming to it from the three major crystals of Atlantis buried beneath Arkansas.

Now we turn our thoughts to these crystals and how to reach the first at Eureka Springs, site of the buried Atlantean Platinum Crystal that exhibits the characteristics of bio plasma -- consciousness and self-awareness. Also, we know this crystal has a deep connection to the Christ.

The journey to Eureka Springs will take several hours because it is at the top of Arkansas. Pinnacle Mountain is near the middle of the state. However, Route 40, a fast good road, will take us to Route 23 which will take us straight to Eureka Springs.

We go along remarking about the trucks. BIG TRUCKS. Most are twice the size of what we would call ordinary trucks, and there are many of them. I wonder who drives these trucks, and after a time, my conclusion is that most of these trucks are probably driven by Arkansas men. Why do I think this?

Poverty is evident in Arkansas. Houses are abandoned and some are disintegrating. My thought is that if a married couple has male children and this married couple lives on a small farm, what would be a source of income when the male children are grown? Probably a small, family-owned farm would not produce enough money for a male child to continue living there after he has grown, married, and had children.

Yes, I think many Arkansas males are driving trucks. And YES, these trucks appear to carry twice as much merchandise as ordinary trucks.

In any case, I note that the truckers are careful drivers and they are attentive to others on the road. They signal their intentions of moving from one lane to another and they wait their turn instead of darting here and there without thought of others.

As we drive along Route 40, I also note that signs bring attention to highways turning off Route 40 to reach different places. But, where are signs telling us that Route 40 will reach Route 23 which will take us to Eureka Springs?

Finally, a few miles before reaching Route 23, one sign does say that this road will go to Eureka Springs. Other routes to other places have more frequent signs.

On Route 23, we quickly realize one reason why the route has not been adequately announced. It is a WINDING mountainous road. I would call this a dangerous road, especially if there is much traffic. Well, today few are using the road. Most are riding motorcycles. Often, four or five are riding their motorcycles together.

It is the weekend and maybe the motorcyclists are not working and are enjoying riding together. At one place, we look from the road to a picnic lunch. About twenty people are eating together.

In any case, the road begins to lose its unsafe characteristics and we are soon picking up speed and going along in a normal manner. When we reach Eureka Springs, we note that it is a lively place with good energy. Yes, we like this place.

Margaret has a special desire to be here. She knows that Thorncrown Chapel, located about a mile from the city, is famous for its unusual architecture. Also, many come here to marry. We realize Thorncrown Chapel may close early, and so, since it is already mid afternoon, we decide to visit this place now.

We take a good highway outside of town and quickly we see a Thorncrown Chapel sign advising us to turn off the main road and go into the forest. Soon we are at this magnificent and very unusual place which is a wooden structure with 423 windows. At the door, a man hands us a brochure with a photograph of the chapel, and just as he is handing us this brochure, a young woman wearing a long, white wedding dress comes to the door to enter. We do not see her husband-to-be, but obviously he is close by. The brochure given to us says this unusual place has won awards from the American Institute of Architecture for being so unusual. We meditate inside the chapel before returning to Eureka Springs.

Now evening is approaching and we do not have a hotel room. And so we phone Hotels.com and within minutes we are given a room at the Express Inn which is near the beginning of Passion Play Road. Instead of first checking in at the Express Inn, we drive to the end of that road to see the towering Christ statue. This is built at the site of Magnetic Mountain, location of the Atlantean Platinum Crystal buried underneath.

In 2013 when we visited, we reached a guard stopping traffic from going to the Christ statue, and we asked if our car could proceed. Yes. We do the same this year, and we receive permission. Good!

A small parking area is close to the statue, called Christ of the Ozarks, and we park our car and walk to the foot of the towering statue. Margaret and I agree that the energy of this statue feels the same as the energy of the towering Christ statue at Rio de Janeiro.

Holy. That is the feeling at both places.

We connect to the crystal energy buried under the mountain and we send this energy as well as the Christ energy to Pinnacle Mountain with the intention that this energy be used to help our planet and its people in a loving, peaceful manner.

We return to the car to drive slowly away from this wonderful place and check in for the night at the Express Inn.

After a night's sleep, we have breakfast in a small room, and here we speak with a man whose family home is at Paris, Arkansas. When we tell him we will be driving this morning to Magazine Mountain, he says he can see Magazine Mountain from the Paris home. He says it will be easy for us to find Paris on a map and then drive to it.

His words are a relief, and after breakfast we throw our few things into the car to begin our journey to Paris. The map shows us that if, from the Express Inn, we follow Route 62 to the west, we should easily reach fast Route 40 that will take us directly south until it turns to go east. This makes sense because our map shows us that Paris is to the east.

But now we make a mistake. Two local men are standing at Route 62 and Passion Play Road. We stop to tell them we want to confirm that just ahead of us we will reach Route 40, the expressway. Do they agree?

No. They say that we must turn around and go the opposite way. And so, with much misgivings, we turn around and begin driving east.

Outside of Eureka Springs, we pass the cutoff to Thorncrown Chapel, and then we read a sign saying we are ready to reach a town called Berryville. Oh dear! This is exactly the opposite of what we want. We are headed the wrong way!

And so we make a u-turn and begin scanning the map for small routes that will take us west and south of Eureka Springs. We have had enough of Eureka Springs for this journey. And yes, we do reach Route 40, and we pick up speed as we go straight south on this expressway. When we are to change direction and go east, we do this.

Now we are looking for a road sign saying we will soon reach the town called Ozark. We know we must turn south on Route 23 before we reach Ozark. We go only a short way and then there is a sign to Paris. GOOD!!! The map is VERY HARD TO READ because of a joining of roads, but we have seen the sign to Paris and WE WILL REACH IT NO MATTER WHAT.

Well, we do reach Paris and the mountain is just ahead of us. We follow a sign to Havana because the road will take us through beautiful, mountain-forest territory.

A few years ago, we visited Mount Magazine, and we remember this scenic route even though we are now driving in the opposite direction of earlier. When we reach an official viewpoint, we stop and look. I am thinking about the enormous Atlantean crystal, the Emerald Crystal having to do with heart energy and healing, and it is buried beneath Mount Magazine. Now we join its energy with its brother, the Platinum Crystal at Eureka Springs, and we send the energy of the two to the Pinnacle Mountain Sun Disc so that this energy will circulate around the world.

The Internet has told me that the name "Magazine" stems from an experience of early French explorers who were at the mountain at the time of a big landslide. They reported that the landslide explosion was so great, the noise resembled an ammunition magazine exploding.

When our journey to the burial place of the Emerald Crystal is finished, we travel on Route 10 straight west until we are nearly at the border of Arkansas and Oklahoma. Here, the route name becomes Route 45. We cross the border to reach the Talimena Ridge where the Atlantean Blue Crystal of Knowledge is buried. We put our minds on its energy and then we combine it with the energy of the other two buried Atlantean crystals to send the combined energy to the Pinnacle Mountain Sun Disc for circulation around the world.

The work with the three crystals is done.

Now we begin putting our minds on traveling to Mount Ida, which some call the "Quartz Crystal Capital of the World". It is located close to Lake Ouachita, and the area is known for its quantity and quality of crystals. There are even private mines that for a fee allow people to search for their own crystals.

A few years ago, when we were at Lake Ouachita, we drove from the lake to the area pertaining to Mount Ida, but we did not enter the town itself. We reached a park that had no visitors, and we sat alone there to meditate and to eat sandwiches we had earlier bought.

Now, three years later, we drive to the city of Mount Ida and the energies feel commercial. We stop at a tourist place to get maps of the lake area and to ask about staying overnight at a resort. Well, we are told the resorts are full at this time of year, and so, if we want to stay overnight, this may not be possible.

To check out availability, we drive to a resort on Lake Ouachita, and yes, we quickly learn that staying overnight at a resort will probably not be possible. The resort where we stop has a sign on the office door saying the resort is full and no one is in the office. If we want answers, we can phone. And so we phone, but no one answers.

We drive to another resort and it is full.

Where will we stay the night?

We drive along slowly and then we hit 'pay dirt'. Beside the road is a ground-floor motel stretching out so that probably there are about fifteen rooms. Are all taken for the night?

Across the road, on a slight hill, is a long stretch of a building, a grocery store. A gas station sits in front of the grocery store.

We need gas. We will stop. We will ask about the motel on the other side of the road.

Yes! Pay dirt. The grocery store, which has tables and chairs for those who want to eat, controls the gas station as well as THE MOTEL ACROSS THE STREET!

Yes. There is a motel room for us, and yes, there is fresh food available in the grocery store for us to order and eat at the store's tables and chairs.

Hurray!

And so, at the end of the day, when we want to 'quit' for the day except thinking about getting gas, eating, and sleeping, we have ALL THREE REQUIREMENTS.

In the morning, the city of Hot Springs plays with our thoughts. This is a famous thermal water place into which comes one million gallons of water per day from forty-seven plus hot springs. Today, Hot Springs continues to be very active with bathhouses for those who desire this healing water energy.

Even earlier, before the arrival of the White Man to Arkansas, some Native American tribes believed in the sanctity of the area. What is called today Hot Springs National Park was called Manataka, meaning Place of Peace.

The Tula people made a triangle of energy of Manataka and Mount Ida and Caddo Gap, their residence.

We decide that today we will energize this triangle of energy. We will bring to life the ancient belief so that, if agreeable, this combined energy can help our present-day Mother Earth and those living on her.

First, we return to Mount Ida with the thought that we are beginning to activate the ancient triangle belief system. Then we go south about fifteen miles to Caddo Gap where we are pleased to see a posted tribute to the Tula people who once lived here.

On this posted tribute is an interesting remark. When the Spanish under the leadership of Hernando de Soto were attempting to occupy the Tula homeland, the Spanish warriors were met by the most fierce fighters they had ever encountered.

To reach the third part of the energy triangle, Manataka (Hot Springs National Park), we drive a bit south of Caddo Gap to reach Glenwood where we begin taking Route 70. This is an excellent, fast road and when we come close to the city of Hot Springs, we watch for signs for Route 7 which will take us to the Hot Springs National Park. We are soon on city streets with elaborate buildings constructed in an excellent manner.

As we drive along, we pass bathhouses and hotels. Yes, this indicates that many people still have a desire to visit this healing waters city. Now we unexpectedly see a sign to Hot Springs National Park. We make a sharp left on these city streets and begin taking a narrow route straight up and into a forest.

A forest in the middle of the city?

Amazing.

A sign tells us we will not be able to turn around. We must follow the narrow route to the end. Well, we are 100 percent willing to follow it to the end. We drive slowly, windows open, breathing in the fresh air from the trees. How amazing it is to drive in a forest in the middle of a city. And, we do not see any walkers or cars. The place has retained ancient energy. WONDERFUL.

And so, concluding this triangle travel to Mount Ida, Caddo Gap, and Manataka (Hot Springs National Park), we are satisfied.

When we reach the other end of the forest and return to city streets, our minds begin to concentrate on driving a few miles to Blue Springs where there is a turnoff to the Jim Coleman Crystal Mines that allows people to dig for crystals after paying a fee. At the mine headquarters, we park facing two astonishing large rocks. We know these rocks come from the interior of a mine because we can easily see indentures, quite a few, where crystals lived before they were extracted.

I sit in the car and look at the astonishing rocks while Margaret goes to the office to enquire about the mining. Here, she can see where people mine in an open pit, not underground. Well, our view in front of our parked car gives us more insight about crystal mining than if we had joined those digging for crystals on the surface.

We leave the mining area and focus on circling Lake Ouachita in order to circle the energies of the lake. We cannot see the lake from the road, but our road has cutoffs we can take to reach it. We try these cutoffs two or three times, but we are too far from the lake to see it, and so we keep returning to the main road. Then we make a mistake. A gravel road we have taken does not return to the main road. Where is it? What can we do? Drive along on gravel roads hoping we will reach the main road.

We decide to be mindful of electric light wires. If they follow the gravel road we are on, then we know that somewhere up ahead there with be civilization. Or, at least a house where we can ask for directions.

Well, now the light wires 'disappear', but there is a house built alone back in the woods. A car is parked near the house. We drive on an unsteady driveway and when we reach the front of the house, we stop and fortunately an elderly man opens the front door and comes out with a puzzled expression on his face. Obviously, not many stop here!

We ask directions to the main road, and after we adjust our voices so his 90% deaf ears can hear us, he explains what to do. GOOD.

We smile our 'thank yous' and drive away, following his directions. When these become vague, we must make a decision on whether to turn here or turn there. We keep our fingers crossed and SOMEHOW we reach the main, paved road. WOW.

A sign soon tells us the mileage to Story, a town on our map that shows us we can turn there on Route 27 which will take us to Mount Ida.

Well, good. That is enough for today. We are hungry and we are tired and we decide to drive to Mount Ida, turn left on Route 270 and go along until we reach the motel where we stayed last night. Will they have room for us? THEY MUST.

And they do.

We buy gas across the road, eat cooked food in the Grocery Store, and that is the end of our day.

This morning we have scrambled eggs and a few other things at the Grocery Store, and then we say good-bye to the kind people and leave.

I want to mention again that the Arkansas people we have been meeting throughout the trip have been kind, considerate, patient, polite. They are like the trees throughout Arkansas. Happy. Mother Earth must be providing the trees with good food. Maybe she isn't feeding the Arkansas people what the trees eat, but the people seem to be eating good stuff.

This morning, our thoughts are on driving to the diamond mines near a place on our map called Murfreesboro. We return to Mount Ida to take Route 27 which will take us there. Of course, our map shows 'a million' routes along Route 27, but we are used to this confusion and we make our way down to Murfreesboro in a quick manner. Here, we take Route 301 to the turnoff to the Crater of Diamonds State Park, and within minutes we are approaching a big parking area that is already filled with cars even though the morning is just beginning.

A few years ago we visited this place and so we know we must enter the Visitor's Center to pay before we are allowed to walk to the actual diamond search site. Paying is quick enough to do, and we are soon walking to a big plowed brown field where people are quietly concentrating on digging for diamonds. Single people are here, and couples, and children with their parents. All concentrating on finding diamonds.

We stand and watch, waiting for someone to bring up a diamond.

The plowed field looks different from our last visit. Earlier, the dug up field was coarse, which would make the finding of diamonds easier. Just now the field is smooth mud because it has recently rained hard.

How often do these people, all hoping to find diamonds, come here to dig?

Young children, probably ages seven through ten, seem used to digging for diamonds. Today, Margaret and I see no evidence that diamonds are being found.

After a time, we have seen enough and we return to the Visitor's Center to look at displays of diamonds. One display has an IMPRESSIVE CLUSTER of tiny diamonds. Maybe twenty tiny diamonds individually sitting next to their tiny brothers and sisters. All are shining as if they had been polished this morning before the Visitor's Center has opened.

We leave the diamond place and begin driving toward Little Rock, knowing our visit to Arkansas is ready to close. Just before entering the city, we take Route 430 North to bypass the city, and then we take Route 40 to reach Route 440. Within a few more minutes of driving, we are on Route 165 to return to the Toltec Mounds to say good-by to the Sirian/Pleiadean/Arcturian Command. We do not make a mistake driving! We do not need to stop and ask for directions!

Hurray!

When we reach the mounds, we enter the Visitor's Center to watch again the short video explaining about the mounds. Near the video screen are three fish living in a tank, and we say good-bye to them. We said good-bye to them during our first trip less than a week ago. They seem lonely and we ask the park manager where was the first home of the fish. He says they were caught nearby. I know no one will return them to their first home and I feel sorry for them. I think they are not happy fish.

Now it is time for us to drive to the airport, which is relatively close. Signs show us where to turn in our little black rental car, and we give him a pat or two when we say good-bye. Then we walk a short way to the American Airlines ticket counter where we are given our tickets for tomorrow.

It is time to phone Hotels.com to ask for a place to stay close to the airport, and yes, that is easy enough to do. Then we stand outside with our bags to wait for a free shuttle. When it comes, we are taken to the Days Inn, and yes, this motel is very close. The woman who runs the place, and who says she herself has a room here to live in, gives us accommodations only three doors from the main office.

Now it is time to eat, but where do we eat? The motel does not serve dinner food, and the only place to eat is a restaurant next door with a sign announcing itself as WAFFLE HOUSE. Waffles are for breakfast, not for lunch or dinner. What should we do?

Well, we go to the Waffle House and we are greatly surprised to learn that this place has EXCELLENT food that has nothing to do with waffles. We eat a hearty meal and we are satisfied!

The waitress, with many smiles, is very kind. We talk a bit with the chef, and he is kind, too.

This chapter closes now and Margaret's chapter on Arkansas is ready to begin.

CHAPTER 8

ARKANSAS

From Margaret:

June 10:

We are up at 4:00 a.m. and Joan, the taxi driver, comes to take us to the airport where we go through Security and wait for our plane to Chicago. In Chicago, we transfer to a small plane to Little Rock. It is a smooth ride and the staff is cordial.

Interestingly, as we were landing, I note there are individual small white clouds quite close to the ground. Are these ships? A welcoming committee?

Hmmmmm.

When we are on the ground, we pick up a rental car and head to Toltec Mounds, the location of the Sirian-Pleiadean command in another dimension.

We drive along and begin to worry that we have gone too far and are possibly lost. Immediately we turn into a liquor store parking area to ask directions from a man coming out of the store. He says we are on the right road and we can follow him. He will show us the way. What kindness.

When we arrive at the parking area for the mounds, we stand under trees by a fence looking at the three large impressive grass-covered mounds in the distance. It is hot, in the 90's, and we enjoy the cool of the shade trees. Now we go inside the Visitor Center and at the suggestion of a cheerful ranger, we watch an excellent film on mound builders.

When the film ends, we go outside to look at the mounds and I begin playing the Blessings Chimes. A mockingbird is singing and the chimes blend in with his singing. I am playing the chimes for the energy field of the mounds that hold underneath the headquarters of the Sirian-Pleiadean command. I am also playing the chimes for the Pinnacle Mountain Sun Disc and the three major Atlantean Crystals brought to Arkansas before Atlantis went down.*

*See Glossary: James Tyberonn references.

We leave the mounds to make our way to the Embassy Suites Hotel where we stayed in 2013. Again we get lost finding our way but we make it.

In the evening, we phone our friend Hideo Nakazawa, a great peace person in Japan. His tradition is to powerfully clap to bring positive energy and healing. As he claps, I focus on the Toltec Mounds, the Pinnacle Mountain Sun Disc, and the Atlantean Crystals.

June 11:

Early in the morning, Barbara and I talk about Arkansas and she says because we are in the frequency of the crystals, the people are happy. The hotel desk attendants are positive and enthusiastic. We see joyful adults and joyful children. We are in the energy field of the Arkansas crystals and our body crystals within us are joyful.

I receive a channeling:

Dear Margaret, you have been given this treasure trove of knowledge which you have in your own system. The key is to throw away the clutter of the mind and proceed with your own seeing, healing and feeling.

Your task is to bring the Blessings Chimes and the Vortexes to fold in the energy of the dolphins, humans, musicians, healers and dreamers with the Crystalline Circle of Energy here in Arkansas. You carry the love crystals -- communication with crystals and plant life and dolphins.

It is a time of balance, joy, upliftment—the enhancement of knowledge, of vitality, of joy, and good-naturedness. The people of Arkansas are true beings. They are upbeat even with the negative news in the media. They are kind, generous, and helpful. Crystal keepers. You cannot have a negative crystal keeper. It will not happen. Look at what happened years ago with the fall of Atlantis. So be of good cheer. Relax into the journey. Everything you do is fine. You cannot get lost because you are here in the Vortex of Crystalline Energy. Frequency of Joy. Frequency of Love. That is all that is required. The rest brings on confusion. Be an open field. Receive and transmit Light. That is all that is required.

Blessings for your journey.

With love from the Cosmic Dolphins

At 8:00 a.m. we check out of the Embassy Suites to drive to Pinnacle Mountain. When we pass St. Margaret's Episcopal Church, I pray to St. Margaret for ease and grace in finding our way to Pinnacle. And yes, we do come to a powerful view of Pinnacle Mountain, home of the powerful world Sun Disc.*

*See Glossary for Tyberonn references.

At the entrance to Pinnacle Mountain State Park we enter the West Summit recreational area and the parking lot is filled with family vehicles. We go to a fisherman boat launch and there are two men going fishing in their kayaks.

I move toward the water to give a greeting and prayers to this beautiful place that we had visited three years ago. I see that all has remained peaceful. The water calm, no wind, no ripples. Just peace.

I bring out the Blessings Chimes to bless the water. When I begin sounding them, I hear a mockingbird singing in tune with the chimes. The water, dancing, seems to make the same sound as the Blessings Chimes and the bird. Delicate. Delicate. Delicate. Crystalline. Crystalline. What a gift to observe the harmony of the water and bird with the Blessings Chimes.

I also ring the Blessings Chimes for the Pinnacle Mountain Sun Disc and all the Sun Discs of the world.

Afterwards, we drive to the Visitor Center where I thank staff member Thea Hoeft for the wonderful directions she gave us on the phone before leaving for Arkansas.

At the Visitor Center's viewing deck which shows me the Arkansas River and wetlands, I begin playing strongly the Blessings Chimes. From here, I also see two tall pine trees coming together making one tree. They are family. The birds are here, too. A whole family of large birds circle overhead. One eagle is circling. We are receiving a greeting.

We are reluctant to leave this wonderful place but we need to travel to Eureka Springs to be in the area of the Atlantean Platinum Crystal. It is a long drive but we move fast on Expressway 40 until we reach Route 23 which zigzags us north through the Ozark National Forest. This route is known as the Arkansas Pig Trail, but this does not mean wild pigs run up the road. It means a shortcut for University of Arkansas Razorbacks sports fans.

We move slowly twisting and turning. Large trees grow over the road to resemble a green cathedral. Majestic views are everywhere.

We have heard this is the favorite route of motorcyclists and we are sharing the road with bikers.

After a while, the road smooths and we easily make our way into Eureka Springs. We stop at what we think is the Visitor Center, but it turns out to be an antique store. The owner, originally from New York State, tells us about Thorncrown Chapel outside the city. This is a surprise to me. I did not know the chapel is here. For many years I have wanted to see it.

We drive to the Chamber of Commerce Tourist Information Center to get maps. Here, a kind couple tells us about the Christ Statue and the religious plays. In fact, the couple we talk to are enthusiastic volunteer actors in the Passion Play. They say 500 people came last night to see the play. When we ask about Thorncrown Chapel, they know it well for they were married there many years ago!!

We want to stay at a hotel near the Christ Statue because it is on Magnetic Mountain, location of the great Atlantean Platinum Crystal. Because we do not yet have a hotel for the night, we phone Hotels. com which books a room for us at nearby Express Inn.

Now we drive to Thorncrown Chapel* about one mile outside Eureka Springs in a densely wooded area on a high bluff. THIS IS AN AMAZING PLACE. I have goose bumps. Not only is the chapel in an exquisite setting, but its open construction has me feeling I am sitting in the trees on a mountainside. The framework is delicate and uplifting, and the walls are glass so the interior is all light. My mind soars with this beautiful site, and I am with all of Nature.

The Christ speaks: *This is my favorite chapel for it has no walls.* I can feel He is well pleased.

*See Glossary: Thorncrown Chapel.

When we return to Eureka Springs, we go to Passion Play Road to drive to the entrance of where The Great Passion Play is held. Here we are stopped by an attendant who asks us what we want to do. We respond we want to go to the statue of the Christ and the attendant happily waves us on.

When we reach the sixty-five foot plus statue of the Christ, we park and walk toward Him. His arms are outstretched, and He is looking over the valley. I think this Christ of the Ozarks has a similar frequency as the Christ the Redeemer Statue in Rio de Janeiro. This one of the Ozarks is on top of the Platinum Crystal deep beneath. We can feel its great power. Again, goose bumps.

I bring out the Blessings Chimes and begin to chime as I stand in front of the statue, looking up at it. The energies of the Cosmic Christ and the Platinum Crystal are with me while the Blessings Chimes are sending this love frequency out to the world.

June 12:

3:30 a.m., I am up early, and my mind is on Eureka Springs, capturing the feeling of this place of rejoicing and radiance. I would like to bottle this and send it out to the world.

I am thinking again of Arkansas being the location of the three great Atlantean Crystals and the site of the world's prominent Sun Disc as well as the Toltec Mounds -- all broadcasting, expanding, healing, enlivening Mother Earth and her inhabitants. We are all one from the smallest atom to the greatest complex of systems. Awakening humans will enjoy the wonder of it all. It is hard for me to sleep.

This morning when I am walking to the car, I see crystal fragments in the road cement highlighted by the sun's early morning light. Oh my, crystals everywhere in Arkansas!

We have been told this morning that we should go to Paris, a town south of us to reach Mount Magazine which is the site of the great Atlantean Emerald Crystal of Healing. When we begin driving, we realize we are driving in the wrong direction. We have been given incorrect instructions. Never mind, it will take a bit of time but we will correct the matter.

The day is bright and sunny. But, clouds slowly build in the distance so that before reaching Paris, the heavens open up and water comes down. A deluge! To our horror, the windshield wipers do not work, so we have to turn the wipers on and off by hand. It is raining so hard I can hardly see. We are in a farming area with rice growing on either side of the road and big ditches flanking the road. We call to the Higher Worlds, Help, Help, Help, and the rain stops. We go to Paris where we ask a man coming out of an auto store how we should operate the wipers. He puts his hand through the open window and pushes down hard on the handle and the problem is solved.

Now we drive to the top of Mount Magazine knowing that beneath this mountain is the Atlantean Emerald Crystal of Healing. The crystal feels very close as we stand at the first lookout viewing the valley and adjacent mountains. I play the Blessings Chimes and I know the delicate sound frequencies are going to the big healing crystal. The sound of the chimes joins with the birds singing and the leaves fluttering. All of Nature responds.

When we are at the top of Mount Magazine, we stop at the Visitor Center to ask about how to reach Talimena Ridge, location of the third Atlantean Crystal, the Blue Crystal of Knowledge.

When we are driving down the mountain, a young female deer steps out of the forest and pauses at the side of the road. We stop to let her pass. Native Americans believe the deer holds healing medicine. How appropriate the deer is on Mount Magazine where the great Atlantean Emerald Crystal of Healing is!

At the town of Magazine, we stop at a gas station to ask where is a good place to eat. Highway 10 Cafe, we are told, is a delightful nearby place.

We stop here and when we open the door, welcoming and enthusiastic people greet us and we sit and order a delicious cheese omelet. We are asked to mark our hometown on the USA map on the wall showing where long distance eaters come to enjoy their food. We are told everyone is welcome.

When we leave, we head west toward the Talimena Ridge, location of the Atlantean Blue Crystal of Knowledge. At the border of Arkansas and Oklahoma, we cross briefly to ring the Blessings Chimes. Barbara and I puzzle over the exact place of the Crystal and Barbara says it is in another dimension and placed at a time when there were no states and state borders. Then I receive from the Higher Worlds: *Sound travels. You are focused on the Crystal and the Crystal knows this.*

Our intention now is to drive to Mount Ida which is in an area where there are major Atlantean crystal beds. Hopefully, there will be accommodations for us. But, as we drive into town there are hardly any motels, hotels, or inns. And so we decide to seek accommodations near Lake Ouachita. At first we find only full resort places, but when we return to the main road, we see Joplin Inn, a motel on the roadside. Is there a vacancy for us? Yes! Not only do we have a room, but we eat a delicious dinner at their Joplin Grocery Store across the road. Everything has worked out perfectly.

June 13:

Margaret musings:

4:00 a.m., I am amused by the motel's shower curtain that has delightful words printed on it in all sorts of fonts:

Peace – Relax – invigorate – energize -- to give vitality and enthusiasm to – renew – stimulate – cleaning – peaceful spa – calm – unwind – leisure – refresh – exhilarate – unwind – calm – to make (someone) tranquil –Tranquil – Leisure – Luxury – rejuvenate – on and on, words repeat down and across the fabric.

These words point to the gifts of the crystalline energy. When I question the word Luxury, the Crystals say:

The Crystals' gift of Light (Lux) is for everyone. Welcome to the crystal world broadcasting positive energy of growth and peace to the world. Mount Ida, Lake Ouachita, Christ Lake –cosmic lake -- access to other realities.

The birds are up singing, waking Nature.

Now Barbara speaks about the suspension bridges we saw yesterday that linked the mountaintops and went everywhere – over the hills and valleys and rivers and streams. This is how the inter-dimensional tunnels were for transporting the crystals from Atlantis to Arkansas. A different dimension was used.

More channeling from the Crystals:

It is like the search for the Holy Grail – you cannot find it, but it is a reality in your thought. In your thought it exists in its own reality. If all is one, then become that. And what is the Grail? The Grail is the frequency of Love. What do the crystals hold? The frequency of Love. The frequency of Light, the frequency of Peace. Peace, Love and Light.

The angels love when people light up with an AH-HA insight, understanding a joyful moment. That is what stimulates the Atlantean Crystals. They love to share their wisdom. They are natural teachers of Wisdom, Healing, and Energizing their inter-dimensionality.

Arkansas, Brazil, Bolivia, California and Bimini are the locations of the Atlantean Crystals transferred in the past to serve Mother Earth and all life forms in the present. Set up a positive framework and all things will grow to fruition – to the maximum of Love and Light.

Light beings hold and transfer Light.

Light beings hold and transfer Love.

Light beings hold and transfer Peace.

With the strong influence of the Crystalline Energy here in Arkansas, people in most part are very kind and polite and helpful to strangers.

It is within their very nature. Arkansas is a complex society, yet existing on a hotplate of powerful crystals that most people do not have a clue about. Strange birds from other places swoop in and peck about the soil and go out. The waters are ruffled for a moment and then become calm again.

This is Arkansas. The more open you are the better it is.

Everyone seeks to be understood and to understand. That is life – the sharing of oneness and universality. Whether with neighbors, strangers, foreigners, off-world visitors or on-world helpers, incarnated now to expand everyone's consciousness.

Here we are in the crystalline task, mission, purpose of being – expansion of Light –- Love -– Peace.

Master Goi, Saint Germain, the Christ, Mary, Bawa, Sai Baba all swim in these frequencies. Turn the crystal and they are there.

Blessings to you, dear Margaret. We love to share these early-morning conversations when you are up and we are always up -- holding, waiting to give out our Light.

Your Crystal Brothers and Sisters of the Arkansas Crystalline Beds.

We fill up on gas and have a delicious breakfast at the Joplin Store across the road from the motel. Bed, gas, breakfast -- all in one location. Perfect.

Today we plan to energize the crystalline energy triangle of Mount Ida, Caddo Gap and Manataka, "The Place of Peace", which today is called Hot Springs. We have read an article about Star People coming to this sacred area and depositing wisdom of the cosmos in a secret crystal cave. We have no interest in investigating a crystal cave, but, we want to circumnavigate the three points of this triangle in order to energize crystalline energy of love, peace, and healing for the Earth.*

*See Glossary: Article on Manataka.

We drive to Mount Ida, the first point of the triangle, and then we go to Caddo Gap, the second point of the triangle, residence of the ancient Tula people. Here we stop to read a posted tribute to these people who strongly believed in peace. We wish to honor this peace. We drive up a road and stop by a lovely pond with a stream near an embankment of trees. Nature is close at hand. The birds are singing.

I ring the Blessings Chimes and the sounds harmonize with the birds singing and the flowing stream. All frequencies merge and are amplified by the influence of the crystals.

11:11 a.m., we feel uplifted by our experience at Caddo Gap and we begin to carry the joy towards Manataka (Hot Springs), the third point of the triangle.

Midway, it begins to rain, then pour. It is so intense we need to pull off the road for a moment or two. Then we struggle onwards and we arrive at the city of Hot Springs at 12 noon. The rain stops and THE SUN COMES OUT. We are in the old historic section of town with bathhouses and grand hotels.

When we see a sign to Hot Springs National Park, we know this is specifically in the area called Manataka by the ancient people. We take a twisty mountain road that is in the forest and three quarters of the way up, we stop at a turnoff to play the Blessings Chimes to energize the triangle of Mount Ida, Caddo Gap and Manataka, Place of Peace.

We know that the crystals in this area enliven the high vision of peace.

As we are descending the forest, a young deer, a doe, comes out of the forest and stands at the side of the road. We stop to let her cross. We honor her presence of honoring The Place of Peace.

Now we journey to the Blue Springs area north of Hot Springs to see about the digging of crystals – the mining aspect. In 2013, we visited Coleman's Rock Shop & Crystal and the mines were closed. Now the Coleman Mines are open and we drive there to see the mining operation, museum and gallery.

Barbara remains in the car, hesitant to become involved with commercialism. I persist and walk into the building and stop at a wide expanse of plate glass windows to look below at a broad view of digging in a big pit. This is what the mining operation looks like here. I have seen enough and I turn away to join Barbara in the car.

In front of the car is a large piece of excavated rock with crevices where quartz once grew. Next to this is a large stone slab with quartz crystals growing on top. Are we seeing how the crystals were grown in ancient times by the Atlanteans? WOW!

I play the Blessings Chimes and we thank the rocks and crystals for their gift of beauty. I know the sound of the Blessings Chimes rings true, picking up the clarity of the crystal and the power of the understanding of this amazing concept. We leave satisfied, knowing we have been given a lesson in crystal construction and growth.

As we leave Blue Springs, we see a golden eagle on the lower branches of a tree.

We drive toward Lake Ouachita to begin encircling it. We call it the Christ Lake of Cosmic Consciousness. Then we become terribly lost, lost, lost. The paved road becomes dirt and gravel, and in some places, the gravel is so washed out, we see only solid bedrock. Later, I realize we are on top of the crystal beds and that is where we were supposed to be!

A driver pulling a large motorboat is coming and we stop him to ask directions. He says we are on the wrong road and to go up to the next intersection where we will find the paved road. But, the next intersection does not show a paved road, and so, we follow telephone lines until they stop. Now we feel MORE LOST.

We see a house built back from the road and we drive to it. An old man comes out and he is quite deaf. Once he can hear what we want, he gives us directions to the paved road. He does ask us why we are here in the back country. We smile.

Off we go and we do find the paved road and a sign to Story, the next town. It is on our map! We are no longer lost. We drive to Mount Ida and then to a recreation area and marina on the south side of Lake Ouachita. With the Blessings Chimes in my hand, I walk to the water's edge to sound the chimes for the beautiful crystalline water of the lake.

The wind picks up to help sound the chimes for the water, for the crystals, for the vision of Peace. Water, crystals, Blessings Chimes, birds singing – harmonies, frequencies, blending together.

What a day! We return to the Joplin Inn and we are given the same motel accommodations as before. We have dinner across the street at the Joplin Store.

June 14:

The weather is moist and misty and we are on the road today to go to the Crater of Diamonds. We drive to Caddo Gap and then to Murfreesboro where we begin looking for signs to Crater of Diamonds State Park. On the way, we pass eight large magnolia trees in one stretch along the road. What an amazing sight!

At the Crater of Diamonds, we go to the plowed fields where families are looking for diamonds. Barbara sits at a picnic table watching them as I head off to the upper part of the diamond field to ring the Blessings Chimes. I sit on a bench under a giant oak tree and I bring out the chimes to ring them softly. First I hold them with my arm outstretched. As I bring the chimes closer to my heart, they become louder and louder. They are responding to my heart frequency of love. The sound is amplified.

When I return to Barbara, I ring the chimes near her. We are two observers acknowledging the miracle of so many diamonds living here.

In the early afternoon we make our way back to Little Rock to stay at the Holiday Inn Express. For dinner we eat at the Kobe restaurant.

June 15:

We have only one more day in Arkansas before leaving and I ask the crystals for the best plan of the day.

Their response: We could sense your pull to Pinnacle Mountain, to the water and to the view of the whole, and your sense to check in with the Toltec Mounds. This would complete the full circle of the Ark.

You have come away with the reality of the State of Arkansas – the poverty, the unity, the kindness of the people – the vastness of the trees and the beauty of the mountain vistas and the rivers and lakes, and beneath the surface powerful beds of Atlantean Crystals.

Arkansas is a generating station of crystalline energy — a state of being where all is based on truth. The society is based on love, kindness and compassion. Arkansas Crystals, the Master Crystals, the waters, the Sun Disc, the Crater of Diamonds have made a strong force field that will grow in power to affect the life forms on the planet, to bring positive energy to human thought forms, to lift the people to a unity consciousness. To divide and split and focus solely on one's self and desires becomes dimmer. Emphasis on positive actions and cooperation will continue to expand and bring heaven on earth.

Enjoy the day with your greater awareness.

With love from the Master Crystals of Arkansas Frequency.

Barbara's message from the Higher Worlds: *Go with the flow.*

After breakfast, we leave for Pinnacle Mountain and we drive straight there without making a mistake. As we are approaching, we see the beautiful pyramid-shaped mountain and we see it again when we leave. Our intention for going to Pinnacle Mountain is to go to the recreational center. When we arrive, we see the park is full even though it is so hot today.

We drive to the boat launch to sit by the water. I ring the Blessings Chimes to honor the Sun Disc here at Pinnacle Mountain and all the Sun Discs of the world.

And now we need to drive to the Toltec Mounds to say a good-bye to the Sirian-Pleiadean Guardians. As we approach, the beautiful Toltec Mounds are in the distance. Overhead, I see clouds in the shapes of dolphins and whales and angels, and I also see clouds disguising the ships of the Pleiades and other worlds.

Good-bye, Arkansas, we love you and every aspect of you.

Now we drive to the airport, and after we turn in our rental car, we walk to the airline ticket counter to check in for tomorrow's flight. We phone Hotels.com for accommodations at nearby Days Inn and then we wait outside for a shuttle ride to the hotel. Waiting is not easy. Heat is a factor. Wow, it is HOT today.

At the hotel, we meet an enthusiastic manager who loves hearing about our experiences going to the Atlantean Crystals. For dinner, we eat across the road at the Waffle House and the food is delicious.

June 16:

Last night we turned on television and we watched news full of fear and violence. The political system in the country seems blocked. No vision of unity is showing.

I ask for channeling and I receive the following:

Welcome to the remains or the reality of the third dimension. On this level, the scenarios appear hopeless. There is no peace. There is no love.

There is no light.

To raise one's frequency is to walk and see the world with joy. It is a blessing to be in Arkansas based on the power of Master Crystals. The people do not interfere with the crystals themselves because the crystals are too deep and too powerful to be affected.

Yes, small crystals are on the surface and people are attracted to them but the big energy front, the crystalline power base of the Master Crystals is growing and expanding with the interactions of the Sirian-Pleaidean base at Toltec Mounds. Also growing in power is the crystalline Sun Disc of Pinnacle Mountain that links to and enhances the other world Sun Discs. Everything you saw in Arkansas is important. You can take any aspect of the Arkansas reality/gift to the country, to the world, and follow that.

The power for positive energy/goodness is held by the crystals. Take each one and follow it and all its aspects and this opens the mind and removes the darkness of despair.

Approach the people with love and gratitude (good will) and they will respond in kind. The core of the people is kindness and generosity.

Pull your attention away from the disruptive mass media that is always singing a sad song or that is always spreading negative news instead of telling good news of breakthroughs in science, education and health. If the birds sang a sad song in the morning, nothing would grow. Trees, vegetables, other life forms would not thrive and flourish.

Let the last note be positive. Your trip was a success. You touched base with all the aspects of the emerging Crystalline Age, with Arkansas leading the way. The Crystalline aspect brings gifts and understanding and is a doorway to other dimensions and contacts.

Thank you, the Crystalline Energy of the ARK.

From Margaret: Thank you, Crystalline Energy of the ARK. It has been a wonderful journey.

CHAPTER 9

NEW YORK CITY

Joint Journals:

First from Barbara:

Chapter One of this book tells you about going to New York City for the Winter Solstice, December 2015.

The last chapter of this book tells you about going to New York City for the Summer Solstice. From Little Rock, Arkansas, we fly to Chicago O'Hare Airport and transfer to the New York City La Guardia Airport. We know the evening is quickly approaching, but light is still with us when we land and we are happy. We jump into a taxi and the driver heads us quickly toward a hotel at 94th and Broadway. He takes us on an East River route because he says it is the quickest way to go, and yes, we do race along with little traffic.

Why do we want this quick trip to New York City? Musician Paul Winter will be conducting a Summer Solstice celebration June 18 beginning at 4:30 a.m.* We like his twice-a-year Solstice celebrations at the Cathedral of St. John the Divine in New York City. For several years we have been attending and just before leaving for Arkansas, we emailed him saying we will be attending this year.

*See Glossary: Paul Winter Summer Solstice Celebration.

And so, this chapter begins by saying that after a short sleep, we are at the entrance to the Cathedral. It is just after 4 a.m. on June 18, and we are so early, we are nearly the first to enter. We know exactly where we want to sit, and we quickly take seats leading directly to the steps going up to the performance stage. At last year's concert, before Paul Winter went up the steps to the stage, he stood knee to knee in front of seated Margaret to send forth to the audience dramatic music from his soprano sax.

Well, this year, without stopping, he goes up and down the steps several times during the two-hour performance. However, when the celebration ends and he is leaving the stage for the last time, he pauses in front of Margaret and shakes her hand. Later, we speak with him.

The Solstice is considered one of the most important times of the year. Depending on where one lives on Mother Earth, the Solstice will be the shortest day of the year or the longest day of the year. This June, we observe the longest day of the year.

To emphasize the dark, Paul Winter begins his program at the Cathedral in complete darkness, 4:30 a.m. His music is somber, off-key, to emphasize the dark.

Here is one important thing to mention. When we enter the Cathedral, we are given a brochure of Paul Winter's Solstice celebration. Inside is a notice written on a black background. "In Memoriam. We dedicate our music this morning to Harambe the Gorilla."

May 28, at the Cincinnati Zoo, a three-year-old child managed to enter the enclosure of Harambe, a 440 pound gorilla. Action had to be taken immediately, and a quick decision to kill Harambe resulted in the death of the gorilla. This news immediately spread around the world, and, as can be expected, the public was shocked. Was there a way to save both Harambe and the child?

Obviously, Paul Winter, a lover of animals, was shocked by the death of Harambe and he gives us a memoriam in his Solstice brochure.

Not long ago, Margaret and I attended a Paul Winter's Solstice celebration listening to tree frogs he had recorded when he visited Puerto Rico. This 2016 Summer Solstice celebration will remain in our memories as a connection to gorilla Harambe's death.

The music in the Cathedral continues with the STRENGTH of darkness. Primitive drums begin to BANG, BANG, BANG!

The audience is quiet -- listening.

Now the music becomes more gentle. And more gentle. And more gentle.

Dawn is coming. Light.

We are seated so that when the light of dawn, the sun rising, begins to come, a stained glass window in front of us begins to show color. Predominately red. The figure of Christ the Savior is in the window wearing a bright red robe, and this becomes brighter and brighter as the sun, the light of dawn, becomes stronger.

We know that a cosmic door will open at the moment of this Solstice and that cosmic energy will enter to help our earth. We living on the earth can send peace energy through the open door to the cosmos. That is our world's contribution to other worlds -- Peace Energy.

May Peace Prevail On Earth and Everywhere Else!

Here is a P.S. to this chapter:

While in New York City, we have enough time to take the metro to the Atlantic Ocean near Coney Island. Here Margaret places Vortexes on the sand just at the water's edge, and she rings the Blessings Chimes for the ocean.

Margaret will now tell you about this moment at the ocean's edge.

From Margaret:

June 16:

Few people are here and it is quiet at the ocean. One distant lifeguard is under an umbrella. The weather is cloudy, misty, with a strong ocean breeze.

The sunlight is faint.

I sound the Blessings Chimes for the ocean and I hold them out to the water. The chimes begin softly singing to the water and the wind blows and picks up the sound. The ocean responds.

Two men with cameras come up and ask about the chimes. I am surprised because usually no one disturbs me, but they are interested and I tell them that these are Blessings Chimes from Australia. The sound is an energy gift given to the ocean. The two men love the concept and they want to photograph the chimes with me holding them.

When they leave, three sea gulls approach to keep me company as I play the chimes for the water. I do this a long time. I know the ocean wants the sound of the chimes, a gift of love and healing for the water and all life forms in the water.

Now I want to draw the Vortex Symbols* for the ocean and I draw them on the hard sand where high tides will come in. Each Symbol is encircled for activation and I speak the name of each when I draw them.

*See Glossary: Vortex Symbols.

I am totally at peace with the ocean and greatly energized by giving the gifts of the Blessings Chimes and the Vortexes.

June 18, 3:00 a.m., I am up before the alarm clock rings to dress and to leave for Paul Winter's Annual Summer Solstice Celebration at the

Cathedral of St. John the Divine. We catch a cab outside the hotel, and it is amazing that a taxi comes up just as we need him. We flag him down and we are quickly at the Cathedral.

Here we pick up our tickets at the box office booth and then we walk to the great nave and sit in the first row in front of the stage. Around the stage are giant Balinese gamelan gongs hanging from wooden mounts made of solid logs. Also, there are seven West African dun-dun drums, as well as a grand piano. Powerful music soon comes from this piano, and we know a nearby huge church organ will soon play powerfully.

The Cathedral is dark. Some lights are temporarily on to help people find seats. We know our seats are perfect because we will see the stained glass window of the red-robed Christ as the dawn of the Summer Solstice comes in at full glory between 5 and 6:00 a.m.

At 4:30 a.m. all lights go out and the Cathedral is totally dark. Musicians begin to play in different parts of the Cathedral – the front nave, the sides, the mid section. I relax in the beauty of the music and the darkness and the anticipation of the Light. During the two-hour concert, I will have the Vortexes and Blessings Chimes with me.

At first the music becomes dissonant, showing the tensions, confusion, disharmony of societies. Then the music becomes harmonious with sweet sounds and vibrations of peace. Magnificent duets are played with complex whale sounds and bird songs. Nature is present.

In the crescendo of the coming of the Light, great gongs and African drums link to the heartbeat, the heart connection of Mother Earth. The piano and the organ bring a dramatic resolution of dissonance. The music brings peace.

At the end of this magnificent performance, the audience is clapping and smiling, and the musicians come forward to stand together and be acknowledged. Paul Winter's granddaughter begins dancing the Irish step dance which to me means that she embodies the world children who will inherit the Earth.

As Paul Winter descends the steps, he reaches out and shakes my hand. What a blessing. I am deeply touched.

We speak to him afterward to tell him we have just come from Arkansas that has wonderful crystals. He mentions the great Arkansas crystal that used to be at the north side of the cathedral nave. Yes, we know this great crystal and we miss it.

When we leave the Cathedral, a full bird chorus greets us singing loudly and joyfully, full of exuberance and joy.

All is a magnificent tribute to the Solstice!!

May Peace Prevail On Earth!!

GLOSSARY

CHAPTER 1: NEW YORK CITY
Paul Winter, musician. http://www.paulwinter.com

2015 Winter Solstice Celebration - A Salute to Brazil.

https://www.youtube.com/watch?v=SbpiKfhtsXw

Peter Seeger, musician. http://www.peteseegermusic.com/about.html

Vortexes and Symbols – See extensive information at end of Glossary.

http://www.starelders.net and http://www.starknowledgeenterprises.com/11-11-symbols/

CHAPTER 2: SERPENT MOUND
Serpent Mound Spring Seed and Water Peace Summit 2016. http://alternateuniverserockshop.com/spring-seed-and-water-peace-summit.html

Constellation Draco. See H.A. Rey book, The Stars: A New Way To See Them.

Judy & Peter Dix, CONTACT: WE ARE ALL ONE.

http://www.interstellardialogues.com

Ross Hamilton, The Great Serpent Mound Book of Wonders & Mysteries.

Hawaiian Reni Aiai Bello. https://www.facebook.com/reni.a.bello

Grandmother SilverStar. http://www.starelders.net/index.htm

CHAPTER 3: AUSTRALIA
David Adams. http://www.dolphinempowerment.com/MarineMeditation.htm

White Eagle. http://www.whiteagle.org/who-we-are/white-eagle-and-his-teaching

---

CHAPTER 4: AUSTRALIA
The Broken Hill Sculpture Symposium.

https://www.yktravelphoto.com/places/the-broken-hill-sculpture-symposium/391

Glenda Green, The Lamb and the Lion. http://www.lovewithoutend.com/Miracle_Story_Lamb_Lion.htm

Musical Rapture. https://www.eraofpeace.org/musical-rapture

Broken Hill Mining & Minerals Museum.

https://www.youtube.com/watch?v=L7GK14ybVXI

David J. Adams. https://soundcloud.com/david-j-adams

White Eagle Lodge. http:/www.whiteeaglelodge.org.au

CHAPTER 6: JAPAN
Soul of WoMen International Gathering, Tokyo, May 13.

http://fujideclaration.org/soul-of-women-international-gathering-tokyo-may-13th/

Symphony of Peace Prayers 2016.

https://www.youtube.com/watch?v=lK0yArNqlPE

CHAPTER 8: ARKANSAS
James Tyberonn. The Story of the Fall of Atlantis *and the Atlantean use of Crystals* Archangel Metatron - *Channeler: James Tyberonn*

http://www.thenewearth.org/The%20Fall%20of%20Atlantis.html

Standing Waves of the Crystal - Vortex ~ Archangel Metatron via James Tyberonn, Posted by Jolan on June 7, 2012.

http://www.esotericonline.net/profiles/blogs/standing-waves-of-the-crystal-vortex-archangel-metatron-via-james

Thorncrown Chapel. http://www.thorncrown.com/architecture.html

http://www.thorncrown.com/photogallery.html

Manataka Article. http://www.manataka.org/page352.html

CHAPTER 9: NEW YORK CITY
Paul Winter, Summer Solstice Celebration. http://www.paulwinter.com/summer-solstice/

Vortex Symbols

Chief Golden Light Eagle and Grandmother SilverStar have given us valuable information on how to use powerful energy fields to help Mother Earth and all that live on her. This information has come from sacred ceremony and the information is available through:

1. Maka Wicahpi Wicohan: Universal and Spiritual Laws of Creator, Star Law Manual of the Galactic Federation. Copyright 1996 by Standing Elk. New Title: The Symbols. The Universal Symbols and Laws of Creation: *A Divine Plan by Which One Can Live*, The Heavenly Hosts, The Servants of Creator.

2. The Vortexes, The Universal Symbols and Laws of Creation: *A Divine Plan by Which One Can Live*, The Heavenly Hosts, The Servants of Creator. Copyright 2013 Revised Edition. All Rights Reserved.

http://www.starelders.net and http://www.starknowledgeenterprises.com/11-11-symbols/

Here is more explanation on the Vortexes and Symbols:

Two Star Law Symbols combined make one Vortex.

The **Vortex of Light, Sound and Vibration** is formed by joining the Symbol of the *Universal Law of Light, Sound and Vibration* with the Symbol of *Spiritual Law of Intuition*.

The **Vortex of Integrity** is formed by the *Universal Law of Free Will* combining with the *Spiritual Freedom of Man*. This is a free will planet and can only operate fully when there is complete spiritual freedom of man. There should be freedom with truth and honesty.

The **Vortex of Symmetry** is formed by combining the *Universal Law of Symmetry* with the *Spiritual Law of Equality*. Symmetry means balance between all things, both spiritual and material. As above, so below. Also, equality between male/female, left/right brain, etc.

The **Vortex of Strength, Health and Happiness** is formed with the combining of the *Universal Law of Movement and Balance* with the *Spiritual Strength, Health and Happiness*. In life one has to be balanced to move forward and also one has to move forward to be balanced. Balance is symmetry in motion. With movement and balance come strength and health and happiness.

The **Vortex of Right Relationship** is produced by combining the *Universal Law of Innocence, Truth and Family* with *Spiritual Protection of Family*. This is also a powerful Vortex of social relationship (based on truth) when the concept has moved from the individual to the group.

The **Vortex of Growth** is formed when the *Universal Law of Change* is combined with the *Spiritual Growth of Man*. Change is a basic tenant of life. With spiritual growth, all things thrive. All things change. Nothing is static. Therefore, both the individual and society need the spiritual growth of man. When humanity grows spiritually, then the Vortex of Growth flourishes. In the natural state, all things grow unhindered. With spiritual growth all things thrive.

The **Vortex of True Judgment** is formed by combining the *Universal Law of Judgment* with the *Spiritual Law of Karma*. All actions should be looked at through the eyes of the *Universal Law of Judgment* so that no harm is done and there is no karma. The latter, the consequences of action, can be turned into dharma, teaching. This law applies socially as well as environmentally.

The **Vortex of Perception** is formed by the combining of the *Universal Law of Perception* combined with the *Spiritual Law of Future Sight*. It is important to perceive the impact of one's actions and to use the gift of future sight. Needed now are planetary actions that affect in a good way the lives of the people in relationship to the air, the water, the land, the life on this planet.

The **Vortex of Connection to Life** is formed with the combining of the *Universal Law of Life* with the *Spiritual Law of Choice*. Life is enhanced by correct choices. It is diminished by poor choices. Therefore, choose wisely. Choice and Life are integrally connected.

The **Vortex of True Nature** is formed by the combining of the *Universal Law of Nature* with the *Spiritual Law of Protection*. Nature exists and thrives. It is up to mankind to protect Nature so that all life thrives on this planet.

The **Vortex of Love** is formed by combining the *Universal Law of Love* with the *Spiritual Law of Healing*. One has to have Love to give healing and to receive healing. Love is the greatest healer. People, Nature, all creatures, plants, cells, molecules, atoms, adamantine particles respond to Love. All have a consciousness. Love creates. Love heals. Love is the highest power of all.

A Vortex is formed at the center of a circle of all Vortexes displayed together. This Vortex is called **Universal Unity and Spiritual Integrity**. All Vortexes bring unity. All Vortexes thrive with integrity. Integrity is the foundation of the Vortexes.

Here is information on a Native American Calendar related to the Symbols.

The EarthStar Way Calendar, A Sacred Cosmic Earth Moon Sun MorningStar Dance with The Seven Stars. The Universal Symbols and Laws of Creation in Day By Day Living.

Printed in the United States
By Bookmasters